# PASSING ON THE WISDOM

# R.O.L.E.
# PLAYER

## JEROME "JUNK YARD DOG" WILLIAMS
### R: RELENTLESS O: OPPORTUNIST L: LEVERAGING E: EVERYTHING

For permission requests, write to the publisher at the address
below, addressed "Attention: Permissions Coordinator."

JYD Project
2831 St. Rose Parkway Suite 203 Henderson, NV 89052

ISBN
978-1-7-7962-626-4 (Hardcover)
978-1-7-7962-625-7 (Paperback)
978-1-7-7962-627-1 (eBook)

Ordering Information:
Quantity sales. Special discounts are available for corporations,
associations, and others who purchase in bulk.

Please contact Johnnie Williams III:
Tel: (360) JOH-NNIE
Visit www.RolePlayer13.com.

Printed in the United States of America

Tellwell Talent
www.tellwell.ca

*I dedicate this book to my greatest gifts.*

IV

# ROLE Player
## JEROME "JYD" WILLIAMS #13

Imagine looking back over your life and seeing a consistent dynamic making up every aspect of yourself. It's taken me more than a half-century to come to the realization and (maybe) the acceptance that I am different. I was different, and I've been different my entire life. Now, all of the funny looks, the whispers, the mockery, and the judgment make a lot more sense. Folks were trying to figure out how I just kept on winning. And trust me when I tell you that life played some fantastic defense.

## *"I was going to claim my birthright, and you can too!"*

My parents often shook their heads (back in the day) because I was so resistant to doing what I was told. However, their system of consistency and positive habit formation helped discipline me to play this game according to its rules. I've come to a place where I feel like Dorthy in The Wizard of Oz. The message and the method were there the entire time; I couldn't see it or wasn't ready to. Well, now I understand and want to pass the wisdom on to you. I've got to tell you how I made it to the NBA without a big name or any local or national ranking. And I made it to the White House for a steak dinner with the president without winning a national championship.

# "So, how did I do it?"

I focused intensely on the R.O.L.E. offered to me, even though it often worked against my strengths and challenged my comfort zone. Throughout the process, I became a *R*elentless *O*pportunist, *L*everaging *E*verything.

## "I played the game, and I'm coaching thousands of future stars to do the same."

This is my story of how I built my NAME, cultivated a philanthropic IMAGE, and trademarked my LIKENESS. So, get ready to catch the pass, as this book has something for everyone.

# Commissioners Comments

by Adam Silver, NBA Commissioner

Jerome Williams' NBA playing career was defined by his hard work, persistent energy, and competitive spirit.

He understood and embraced his leadership role on every team he played for. But his impact extends far beyond what he accomplished on the court and in the locker room. From serving on the Executive Committee of the National Basketball Players Association to his involvement with NBA Cares and our Basketball Without Borders program to interning at the NBA league office, Jerome has relished the opportunity to impact communities through basketball.

He has also served as a mentor to generations of players who have sought his advice on how to navigate their own careers in basketball and business. Jerome was the perfect role player and continues to be a fantastic role model and ambassador for our sport.

*"Through personal stories from his NBA career, Jerome Williams shares valuable lessons on what it takes to be the ultimate role player."*

Adam Silver, NBA Commissioner

# My Acknowledgements

by Jerome "JYD" Williams

I am grateful to have created a beautiful family with my MVP and wife of over 25 years, Nikkollette Williams. You have done an excellent job of managing our home. I must stop and say "thank you." What we have accomplished as parents and partners continues to produce outstanding results.

I must acknowledge my children, Sherae, Gabrielle, Giselle, and Jeremiah. You each have brought me so much joy and fulfillment. As I look back to the moment, I decided to walk away from the game that offered me so much; it was to ensure that each of you could grow up with me at home and that I could take you to school each day. I never wanted to continue pursuing my dream at the expense of hindering you all from reaching your own.

My deepest appreciation must go to my first coaches, who created the ideal system for me to grow and dream. Dad, you poured your love and passion for basketball into me, and your high expectations have helped me achieve so much. And Mom, your loving nature inspired me to celebrate and support my many teammates and share what you gave me with others.

I want to thank my older brother Johnnie, who inspired the creation of 'ROLE player' and sharpened my vision for passing the wisdom. You were my writing coach and served as the best accountability partner I could have had throughout my career. You have been by my side the entire time and through the many seasons of my life. I appreciate you tremendously. I want to thank Anthony Muli Mwau for collecting and composing content for 'ROLE player'.

I must acknowledge the man who made me a big brother back in 1984. Josh, thank you for preparing my Hall of Fame application.

I was honored to read the comments from Adam Silver. As a retired NBA veteran, receiving your support was humbling and appreciated. I continue to value the friendship we have built over the years.

I also thank my old friend Marc Spears, an NBA analyst for ESPN. We spoke about 'ROLE player,' and he was willing to write an amazing forward that shares an interesting story about how we met. I respect his accomplishments in the sports media industry and feel fortunate to have his contribution and support.

# COURT of CONTENTS

## My 1ˢᵗ Role: Family Time  19

I can remember my first role, which I had to grow into and learn how to play my part and manage my responsibilities. With lots of love and some very high expectations, my parents helped mold me into the man that many have come to know.

## My 2ⁿᵈ Role: School Days  27

My role as a student-athlete later served as the prerequisite for all my emerging opportunities. I had to learn from the many challenges presented to me, both on and off the court. This was the first game I had to win, and the main message passed on to me was to remain teachable and coachable.

## My 3ʳᵈ Role: Pay to Play  39

My junior college years introduced me to personal accountability and team leadership roles. It was during this time that I grew into a body that would open some doors. But nothing was handed to me, and there was a high price to pay.

## My 4ᵗʰ Role: The Right Answer  49

After choosing to attend Georgetown University, I remember coach John Thompson passing the wisdom, practice after practice. He told me he would teach me how to become a role player at the NBA level, and I will be forever grateful to him.

## My 5<sup>th</sup> Role: 1996 Draft  61

When I heard the NBA commissioner, David Stern, say, "With the 26th pick in the 1996 NBA draft, the Detroit Pistons select Jerone Williams." I knew my life was never going to be the same. What would my new role ask of me?

## My 6<sup>th</sup> Role: Detroit Days  69

As a rookie, I had a lot to learn about the business of basketball, its levels, and its unspoken rules. The staff greeted me with open arms and reserved a seat on the bench. My initial role was to stop pouting and begin to bring the energy I would become known for.

## My 7<sup>th</sup> Role: Toronto Trade  78

I remember getting the call and sitting on the team bus in shock. I didn't know what to feel. It was kind of like being exiled from your friendship group. While in a state of shock, I made a rash decision that cemented my legacy in Toronto and across Canada.

## My 8<sup>th</sup> Role: Chicago Layover  89

I could have stayed at the airport for as short a time as I spent in the windy city. Just as I was thawing out and getting used to the city, my phone rang, and I got word that it was time to pack my bags again. But this would be my last time.

## My 9<sup>th</sup> Role: Guarding the Garden  96

I was honored to play my last year of NBA basketball on one of the world's most significant stages. The feelings generated by Knick fans cheering and actually barking at me after a great play will forever echo in my heart. I never knew who might be in our front row.

## My 10th Role: Early Retirement  105

The most challenging shot I ever took was my last one; if I knew it would be my last, I might've gone out on a three-pointer or one of my classic dunks where I'd hang from the rim.

## My 11th Role: Shooting For Peace  118

The most impactful role I played during my NBA career was that of a role model to hundreds of thousands of youth worldwide through my JYD PROJECT and role as an NBA Global Ambassador alongside Big Bob Lanier. We filled out some passports.

## My 12th Role: Passing The Wisdom  128

The greatest gift I can share with young fans is my time. My post-NBA career has afforded me lots of time to speak with students and adult staff who love asking me great questions about my journey. My message is to "play your role,"

## My 13th Role: Let's Talk NIL  143

I can hardly describe the feeling of finding something to get passionate about that brings back that high-stakes pressure and game-day jitters. To open up the USA Today newspaper more than 19 years after stepping off the court and reading a two-page article about your big shot at helping other athletes leverage their Name, Image, and Likeness (NIL) was an amazing feeling.

## The Legends Speak  153

Imagine sitting back as legends from the past share their thoughts about you, your game, and your contribution to the culture. I have got to let you read some of the comments that greats like Dr. J, George "Ice Man" Gervin, and Allen "AI" Iverson shared with me.

## Growling In Gratitude

After crossing the half-century mark and looking back at all the roles I've been honored to accept and thrive within, I must fully display the role that has opened more doors and won me more friends than enemies. The role that gratitude plays in my life and has played throughout my career had and did make all the difference.

## The Family Business

This unfolding story is far from over. So, the best way to share what I'm up to and see how our next generation is stepping into their greatness was to launch a new TV show titled "The Family Business." It promises to be funny, inspiring, and packed with nuggets of wisdom we'll be passing on. I'll be taking the snapshots from my life and converting them into engaging episodes for fans and families to enjoy.

# The Pre-Game

by Johnnie Williams III

# THE PRE-GAME
Johnnie Williams III, The Encouragement Specialist

As we began this journey as brothers, who would have thought that the balls we played with would bounce us from community to community? We have seen the world together and found ourselves in the company of its most influential people. Our purpose to serve and support others has been an amazing experience. I was honored when you entrusted me with helping you assemble this puzzle. Each chapter highlights your unbelievable story, filled with so many accomplishments.

I felt your genuine intentions for revealing the most pivotal moments within your life so that others might benefit. I find it mind-blowing how our words emerge into our existence. You said when we were just children, "I will play in the NBA," and that manifested into a 26th pick of the infamous 1996 NBA draft class. I also remember mentioning in 2005 that your work off the court would sustain your relevance for 20 years or more. Now, here we are in 2025, serving together (again) on the creation of 'ROLE player.' And, still, we remain focused on *passing the wisdom* to anyone willing to catch it.

I wanted to share an example of the legacy and impression your genuine acts of service left on others. I sent a message to the former Detroit Pistons VP of Player Programs and Community Development. I asked Rex Nelson if he would like to share any comments about you. Now, consider the fact this relationship spanned from 1996 -1999. Rex had this to say:

> *Johnnie,*
>
> *Here are some of my thoughts about both of your influences on the Pistons organization and the Detroit community. Jerome arrived in the 1996-97 season, which was about halfway through the completion of our PARK Program, an $11,000,000 project. It was a Piston' s-led collaboration with the City of Detroit, which involved building and renovating 33 parks throughout the*

*city. One of the key components was leveraging our player involvement to further engage the community stakeholders. Jerome made more free appearances than any other player during his time with the organization. In addition, he was simply down to earth, easily accessible, and truly committed to seeing kids improve their chances for success in life. His approach to this mirrored his "Junkyard Dog" moniker. He worked as hard in the community as he did on the court. His support from his brother Johnnie's unprecedented financial literacy program was impactful and received national attention as it helped students, and in some cases, their parents, learn the importance of establishing good credit, opening bank accounts, and understanding how money works.*

*Johnnie was one of the few siblings, during my 11-year tenure with the organization, that came in and helped their brother's transition into the league. As the older brother, it was clear that he had Jerome's best interest in mind and that he brought vision and skill sets to the table that helped elevate Jerome's presence in the community and throughout our organization. Often, the siblings are dependent and not well-versed in how corporations work. However, it was just the opposite with the Williams brothers, and that was refreshing for me and my staff.*

*Rex Nelson*

# POWER FORWARD

by Marc Spears, ESPN NBA Analyst

# POWER FORWARD
## Marc Spear, ESPN (NBA) Analyst

For two decades, San Jose, California, was the only city I had ever known. And then I went to the U.S. Post Office to get my first change of address card. I was moving to Washington, D.C., to accept a full basketball scholarship at a Division II HBCU called the University of District of Columbia. To accept a full basketball scholarship after two years of playing at a juco was exciting. But to say I was homesick after a couple weeks was an understatement. Being broke, living in a one-bedroom apartment with two other teammates, and lacking food didn't help either.

So, on this particular Sunday of Labor Day Weekend in 1992, I was supposed to be in New York City visiting a new lady friend. But those plans fell through. Story for another day. So even my attempt to take a break from my new environment by going to The Big Apple for the first time didn't work. To make matters worse, a few days earlier, I was disrespected by a grocery store clerk when asked where I played college basketball. When I responded UDC, she said, "Oh, the university of dumb children?"

So, back to this particular Sunday, I wasn't in the best mood in the world to play the game that brought me to D.C. in the first place. The game of basketball. So, instead of being at home or church, I was at the storied "Doc's Gym" with the rest of my teammates playing pickup basketball. I never knew Doc's real name, but he was an affluent local African-American doctor who used to set up these pickup games for college basketball players in the DMV and actually set up all the teams.

So, on this gloomy day mentally, this slender forward named Jerome Williams was on my team. This local kid was just a freshman, and I was 20 years old. I didn't know who he was until I saw him play with the energy of a group of kindergartners at recess on a nice day. But after a couple of games of me and my poor demeanor going through the motions and us losing, Jerome pulled me to the side and said, "Hey man, do you want to play or not? I've seen you play. I know you're better than that. I'm trying to win."

For a fleeting moment, I was somewhat offended about some true freshman trying to check me. But truth be told, he was right. I was a little embarrassed by his challenging words and immediately snapped out of it. I told him I was going to pick it up. And I did. I played with some heart and enthusiasm the rest of the day. And we won.

This was JYD before he became the Junkyard Dog. This was some teenager that Georgetown head coach John Thompson understandably fell in love with that had a gear that most basketball players never mustered the energy to have. This kid was different.

Jerome wasn't the most skilled player for Georgetown. He didn't have height like Patrick Ewing, either. But if basketball players could have played with a hard hat, he should've because he did all the dirty work. Dive for balls. Got every rebound. Made a living off putbacks. Loved defense and shutting down his opponents. A born leader. And boy, was he fun to watch on a fast break while getting a dunk. Jerome did all the dirty work that wasn't on the stat sheet.

From that day at Doc's Gym, I always made a point to watch him during his Georgetown games. I wasn't surprised to see him get drafted in the first round in the NBA in 1996. And it was poetic for him to get the nickname "Junkyard Dog" from his Detroit Pistons teammates that stuck around after his nine NBA seasons. In fact, the "JYD" nickname is still very much alive today, as Vince Carter mentioned during his induction speech in 2024 at the Naismith Memorial Basketball Hall of Fame.

Jerome and I were reunited when he was playing for the Pistons during the 1999-2000 season. That was also my first year covering NBA basketball as a sportswriter following the Denver Nuggets as a beat writer for The Denver Post. I made a point to say hello to Williams when the Nuggets played the Pistons, and he said he remembered our initial meeting at Doc's Gym. Jerome was never an NBA All-Star, nor did he ever average over 10 points per game in a season, but his mastery of the intangibles kept him in the league for nine seasons.

Thirty-plus years later, Junkyard Dog and I always have a laugh about our DC pickup ball story when we see each other. He always loves me to tell it, too, and smiles while re-living it. And despite being

20 years removed from playing in the NBA, Jerome still is heavily engrained in the fabric of the league as he is always around whether it's at NBA games, USA Basketball events, summer league, the Naismith Memorial Basketball Hall of Fame, etc.

Why? He's widely respected. That is what hard work gives you. That is what Junkyard Dog was all about when I met him at Doc's Gym and what he is about today.

- Marc J. Spears, Senior NBA Writer ESPN Andscape
- 2023 Naismith Memorial Basketball Hall of Fame winner of the Curt Gowdy Award for print.

# My 1<sup>st</sup> Role: Family Time

*"I was born an ordinary child but raised to become extraordinary."*

I remember my first role, which I had to grow into. I had to learn to play my part and manage my attitude and responsibilities. With lots of love and some very high expectations, my parents helped mold me into the man that many have come to know.

When I look back at my career and reflect on the person I have become, I realize that my home and my family were the most significant inspirations. Others might assume the Junkyard Dog image and style of play emerged from a collection of elite basketball programs. And that would be a fair assumption.

But no... It was the unseen things that made me. All the ups and downs left me to figure out how to get back up or if I would decide to do so. Some reporters have asked what inspired me and what drives my desire to keep winning. When I would say family, there was often a surprised look on people's faces. I had a dad in the home to model myself after, who expected me to meet each day and every opportunity with a positive attitude. I made it without attending camps or receiving any elite training. I was born on May 10, 1973, as Jerome. I was the second son and the little brother to Johnnie, who was just one year older. My parents are one of those love stories where a guy meets a girl, falls in love, gets married after high school, and has a wonderful family. However, growing up, their lives were nothing like a fairytale. My father had an absentee father, but not because his dad didn't want to be there. He came back

19

from World War II with tuberculosis. Because of this, he could not be around his children, so he separated from his family to protect them.

He missed his father growing up, and it weighed on him. It's also what refined his vision for the future. My father declared that he would always be there and accessible to his family. To my benefit, he stayed true to that throughout my childhood, significantly impacting my brothers and me. He was there when I was playing outside and cheering me on at every sporting event. My dad was a consistent supporter of my dream, and he put in the time to coach me. Most importantly, he demanded I pick my head up whenever I lost.

My father wasn't a quitter and was not raising me to be one. I can remember him often saying, *"When you start something, I want to see you finish it, even if you find that you don't like it."* That was really tough sometimes because, as a kid, you're wired to want to try so many different things. And he supported my interest, no matter what it was, but I just had to keep in mind that I could not stop until it was over. This taught me to stick with things and work with people long enough to see the mission through.

My father was just different, and folks could see it everywhere we went. His passion and positive attitude were evident, along with his desire to inspire everyone around him to be better. He had this drive that he was not going to lose, and he didn't stop trying until he did. It was like he was a superhero doing things many dads could do, but many of them opted to avoid. As I got a little older, I learned more and more about the man I called Dad.

Life had dealt him a bad hand when he was about three years old. After receiving his polio vaccine, he was among the population of children who contracted the disease. It began attacking his arms and legs, leaving him crippled. Or so people thought...

Many may have surrendered to this horrific fate and accepted their unfortunate circumstance, never breaking free from the metal braces that limited their ability to run... I can only imagine the challenges he encountered as a young boy who didn't have his father present to push and support him, as he was doing for me. But that is what provoked his drive. The same fire he helped me find during tough challenges that I felt was more than I could handle. He taught through his example (not suggestion) that what I assumed to be impossible could be overcome with a strong mindset.

I never saw him tearing anyone down, and I never saw him fail to stop and pick someone else up. He had been teased and bullied, but he never let it inspire him to become one as he grew into his six-foot, five-inch frame. He had developed character and mental toughness. He pushed past all his challenges and challengers until he could walk again. But he did not stop until he could jog and run well enough to train me on the court.

> *"I learned to have a strong mindset from my father. I have him to thank for showing me that anything is possible when our minds believe it."*

I think my dad gained his strength from his mother, who was determined to have a good life and made up her mind to attend college. At that time, only four to five percent of Americans had a college degree. It was no easy feat to achieve, especially as a woman during the early 1940s. This revealed to me that she and my father were achievers. They had won championships in life, which allowed them to model self-confidence and the byproduct of determination.

As for my mother, she was raised in a big family made up of six boys and six girls. Her mother stayed home and took care of the children while her dad, who was a decorated military man, ran the family business Ballard Construction. He achieved great success as a result of his *Dedication, Determination, and Discipline*. His strength and bravado were the cornerstones of his personality and identity. He inspired me to reach for success.

My mother was the fourth child, and as more and more siblings began to arrive, there wasn't a lot of focused attention directed at her. As she completed the 8th grade, she and an older sister were sent away to boarding school. But this wasn't your average school; it was one where the children of politicians, sports figures, and entertainers sent their daughters.

In such a school, the young ladies were disciplined by nuns and expected to achieve academic success and master mental toughness. She thrived in that environment and still has her school yearbook to prove that she was popular and a part of every social club and activity.

> ## *"These are some of the social qualities she passed along to me. My mom is responsible for my JYD personality."*

My mother always expected the best from us. It didn't matter whether we were cleaning our room, putting away toys, washing dishes, or sweeping the floor. Her standards were set high, but (first) she taught us how to live up to the higher expectations. She saw it as a way to give us an edge in life. And she would often tell us, "*You will never stand out in the crowd if you do things just like everybody else.*"

Over the years, I have spoken to some folks who wonder how I developed the mindset, discipline, and resilience to keep working on my game (aka myself). I suggest looking at my parents and then looking at their parents (my grandparents). I am just a by-product of each of them. Regardless of the hand, the world dealt to them, they each adapted before adopting a mindset that set them apart. They committed themselves, stayed focused, kept disciplined, and worked hard to turn life's lemons into lemonade.

I became the man I am today because my parents instilled in me the values that helped them turn their lives around. The life principles they modeled have helped me manage and keep my career on track. But I think their greatest lesson was teaching me to step into my role and learn to perfect it, even when I didn't want to accept it.

We had routines and processes to follow that kept our lives organized, and they kept their standards high. We were obligated to display respect and follow their instructions. For example, we would not wake up to play all day just because we were kids and somehow felt entitled to it. We were taught that the world did not owe us anything and that we were not entitled to get it without earning it. But their love was always unconditional and consistent as they supported our efforts.

To earn a ride down to Washington, DC, we needed to complete our homework and the chores we were assigned. Failure to meet these standards would result in no park visits. It was not punishment or our parents being unfair to us; it was a valuable life lesson to put in the work to earn what we wanted. My parents allowed us to manage what we could do and expected that we would do it well.

I was not to quit if assigned a role and found it difficult. No task would be taken back simply because you couldn't do it. If I encountered anything complicated, my parents would provide guidance and work with me to improve it. I would then do it repeatedly until I was good at it. I could only graduate to a more significant role after successfully managing what was already asked of me. This is how my parents helped us develop resilience.

> *"These 'life drills,' as we would later name them, taught me that practice is the cornerstone of improvement."*

Our parents taught us the importance of responsibility. To instill these values, they gave us roles to play. They would not clean up after us; once we were given that responsibility, it was ours.

"You make your bed," my mother would often say. Even though my bed was neat, she used the term to suggest we organize our lives. And making our beds meant taking responsibility for our own lives. Picking up toys, doing homework, reading extra books, or completing chores was practice.

Our beds served as a life metaphor. She was teaching us that it was our choice whether we lay on a bed we made or in a mess we had failed to clean up. A messy and disorganized life was a bed that we chose not to make.

The lessons I learned from making my bed have saved me from many mistakes. They helped me forge the habit of focusing on the little things that produce big results. My family was the first team that assigned me a role. My parents were my first coaches, and they have won and lost with me. But the outcome never determined the way they dealt with us. They consistently demonstrated unity and love for one another (first) as they guided, protected, and provided.

There were very few down days at our home. We were a team, and we chose to be there for one another whether we felt like it or not. That's the idea of consistency; you do the right thing whether you want to or not. I had and still have some of the greatest cheerleaders on the planet. Even to this day, I ring their phone if some good news comes. I am immediately placed on speaker phone so they both can hear what new blessing they'll celebrate or what challenge they'll coach me through. That means a lot!

## *"One of the greatest gifts I ever got was my Dr. J slam-dunk hoop."*

But, besides all the life coaching my parents offered, I must acknowledge the gift that might have held the greatest value. I was about six, and my parents noticed my interest in basketball and admiration for the legend Dr. J. That Christmas, they placed a basketball hoop under the tree. But it was not just a regular hoop but a "Dr. J" Julius Erving's slam-dunk basketball hoop. I cannot even tell you how much that meant. And from then on, my mind was made up; I would become the Dr. J of my day. Who knew what this seed of destiny would manifest into?

They would watch me play for hours, and I would always shout at them, yelling, "Did you see that?" They would clap, cheer, and yell back, "Yeah, we saw that. Go, Jerome!" In my mind, I was already playing in the NBA. I just had to beat my brother first...

## My Mission:

During this chapter of my life, my role was laid out so that I could learn the basics of being a part of a team and understand that I would have to work for the things I wanted in life.

## My Methods:

My parents' daily expectations for me served as the building blocks for future success. Their intentions were to form positive habits that would make doing the hard things more manageable because I was given a system to work from.

## My Measurables:

At this point in my story, I'd say the measurables benefitted my parents in that they didn't have a messy home or disrespectful kids running around crazy. They were creating the life they wanted and an ideal home environment where everyone could thrive, grow, and find peace.

# My 2<sup>nd</sup> Role: School Days

*"It's a great feeling to have others believe in you, but when you lack self-belief & self-love, it is just fool's gold."*

I know now that the roles I played as a student-athlete were the prerequisite for all the opportunities and success that have come. The many tests and quizzes challenged me on and off the court. It was a daily game I had to win, and the lesson I took from it was to remain teachable and coachable. It took a little while for me to grasp that concept because I was a bit stubborn. As adolescents, we sometimes must manage aspects of our personality that work against us.

For instance, all my energy on the court would have to be contained while I was in the classroom. There would be no barking or boxing out teachers. And I wouldn't be in class long if I got caught slamming my trash, nor if I high-fived everyone raising their hand with a question. My school days taught me that timing was everything and that passing tests under pressure was like hitting my free throws with the game on the line.

Early on, my parents made many sacrifices to pay for Johnnie and I to attend private school. I believe they did this to keep us in an environment aligned with the values they taught us at home. This continued until I was seven and Johnnie was eight. Buckets of research say that whatever a child is exposed to until this age will shape their personality and lay the foundation for the future they'll create or experience.

# *"Give me a child until he is seven, and I'll show you the foundations of the man."*

-Aristotle

With an intuitive knowing, my parents placed us into Montrose Christian School, where NBA Champion Kevin Durant would later attend. This school was expensive, and the tuition placed an additional strain on them. But we had no awareness of this; we were just happy kids attending what many would call a privileged school. They kept us there until we both completed the third grade. We were already an entire grade level ahead when we transitioned to our local public school.

The real learning curve for me was adjusting to the change in the school culture and environment. Some kids were cursing, and others were teasing one another during recess. This was a different game. At Montrose, they were big on teaching us how to treat others and spent time explaining why we must respect our teachers. At my neighborhood school, we were more so expected to remember what was right. I had already been taught many of the foundational things.

However, I watched some of my new peers heading to the office for failing to do what our teachers expected. In my opinion, we must coach our young students on how to display the roles expected of them. Then, we must take time to model and practice the execution of it, just like we do with sports.

I didn't recognize the impact this had on my perspective at that time. But later in life, in certain situations, I could tell whether a person I was encountering had been taught by someone or just told what to do. So maybe we need to look at how we are coaching our young people to act and treat others. We absorb what we see and become shaped by our experiences. My parents waited to transfer us after we were seven, so our personalities were more cemented. Therefore, the influence of peer pressure was not so disruptive. Falling short of adult expectations was not going to erode our esteem; rather, it would drive us to improve.

I was taught to imagine myself as an unsharpened pencil. My role each day was to sharpen my skills so I could write my dreams into existence. The school day (like sharpening a pencil) was a grind, and it exposed the most unfocused individuals. My spirit wanted to play, but I had to stay focused if I wanted doors to open for me. I want you to consider the little eraser on your pencil as a reminder of how few mistakes you get to erase. So, get busy taking notes, write down your goals in a dream journal, and track your progress.

Believe me when I tell you, I didn't always do what I just suggested. However, I still reached my dream and want our youth to achieve theirs. So, what did I do that made a significant difference for me? I remember being a third-grade student who cared little about anything besides playing sports. I was not very interested in my classes. I sat through them, just watching the clock and hoping it would tick faster so we could get to recess. That was my favorite part of the day because I got to play with my peers. I looked forward to my moments of freedom! And my teacher must have been observing this because she used what I liked to shift my perspective.

*"She helped me find the competition in being the fastest reader and maybe even the quickest problem solver."*

She didn't judge me by my carefree attitude. I was just a young boy who needed to be inspired. I was a good student who didn't bully or disrespect anyone in school. So, she made it her mission to connect with me. I can't recall everything she did, but her accomplishments helped me see that learning was my responsibility.

She taught me I could compete in the classroom, just like during gym time. She helped me by challenging me to become her fastest reader and maybe even the quickest problem solver. This guidance was a game changer, and it helped me to shift my focus towards competing in class. I still considered anything between me and playing outside, including schoolwork, as an obstacle. So, one day, after another one of our discussions about unfinished homework, I told her that I did not need school.

After all, I was going to be a successful basketball player. What good would English do for me then? Mrs. Steutes might have never had a third-grade student display such pride and ignorance in all her teaching years. She didn't let it show if she was shocked, as she maintained a calm demeanor. It was frustrating as I counted on her reaction. So, I continued to show up with unfinished homework as a silent protest that got no reaction. But then came the day she informed me in front of my classmates that she would be calling my parents.

It would become one of my most stressful evenings, just waiting for the phone to ring. I was hoping my teacher was bluffing, or that she would not make that call. However, at around six thirty, the phone rang. It was Mrs. Steutes, and I began to sweat, watching my mother get filled in about my behavior. "Jerome Vernon Williams," she called out.

I responded quickly, hoping that might earn me some mercy. She called for my dad and told him everything the teacher said. That night, I received some special attention that was bad—and maybe good—in that it re-aligned my priorities and set me back on the right path. When I got to school the next day, I did my homework and all the incomplete work as well.

Was I mad at my teacher for reporting me? Yes, however, I would realize that what she did for me was an act of love and care. She saved me from slipping through the cracks and falling behind. My attitude began to change as I improved in her English classes. I even took an interest in reading more books, too.

From then on, I chose to become a good student, putting more effort into my studies. I submitted my work on time and passed my tests. Things started working out for me, and I began to earn school awards like honor roll and perfect attendance. Moreover, I realized I could play and still be a good student. Many of my teachers would go on to say that I needed my education. But her words have stayed with me over the years.

# "There are moments that help to shape your life, and this, I believe, was one of the shift points where the adults each played their role."

I grew up when you didn't want your parents to hear about your poor behavior at school or around the neighborhood. So, I did what I was told in school so I wouldn't lose my chances to play outside later. My parents would hold my attention by leveraging my love for playing basketball. This inspired me to remain on point, get my chores done, and do well in school. I feel that basketball was also a bridge to stay connected to Johnnie and me.

Because our parents were only twenty years older than us, they were able to challenge us on the court well into our teens, and beating my dad in a game became the ultimate goal for us. My father made time to play two-on-one after school. It may have seemed like another game between a father and his sons for fun, but this was practice. My dad played us like it was an NBA finals game, and if we did win, he would immediately insist we play a best-of-three series.

By the time I entered middle school, I was determined to be the best student and also make it onto the seventh and eighth-grade basketball teams. Once I got to seventh grade, I was excited to try out for our school team. I had worked hard on my game and spent most of my free time on the court. There were about sixty-five kids at the tryouts. Only twelve would be lucky enough to make the team. After the first day, thirty of us made it to the shortlist. I was among them, and it felt good. I continued to do my best, and on the final day, I was confident that I would make the team and represent our middle school.

At the end of the practice, the coach shouted, *"Hey, you guys have made it very hard for me. Practice starts tomorrow for those who made the team. If you got cut, keep working on your game."* Then, he posted the names on the board outside the gym. I felt no need to rush to it, assuming that I was on that list for sure. My friends Irfan and Jamil came to tell me that I had been cut. I replied, "I know I'm on the team." My friend Chico was one of the seventh graders who made the team. If he had made it, I should have, too. I felt that I was a better player. I entered my coach's office like there was a problem. I thought it was some mistake and couldn't wait for everybody to leave the area. My face reflected desperation, and he asked me what was wrong. I explained there was some mistake.

"My name is not on the list, coach." He replied, *"Well, I can tell you why. You were one of the best players but had no left hand."* I never thought I needed to develop my left hand to be a good player. I responded, "I'm much better than the people you selected." He replied, *"Those people can go both ways. That makes them more valuable."* What I saw as rejection and failure was a moment that would change my approach to practicing for good. It would influence me to make changes and, in his words, more valuable. He pointed out a weakness I could fix and all the inspiration I needed to improve.

From that day on, I trained to play better with my left hand. I tied my right hand to my hip so I could force myself to only use my left hand. I did short and long drills, and I practiced in every possible way I could until I made that weakness a strength. It changed everything for me. I was becoming a better player, but I mostly went unnoticed. My parents transferred me back into another private school for my eighth-grade year, where I played against and with some really smart students who were not so good on the court.

My time at the Woods Academy might not have played a significant role in my basketball skills development, but it did something else. I was able to befriend peers who went home to houses that looked like small schools. Some of my friends lived in homes with swimming pools and full basketball or tennis courts in their backyards.

Seeing this began to plant in my mind that this life was possible, and I saw two ways to get it. Their parents were just really smart people, not pro athletes, and they either owned a business or were leading someone elses. This is what helped me see the student coming before athlete. I knew I would have what they had by becoming an intelligent athlete. I continued to play daily with my dad and brother

Johnnie. Some days, we would play ball in areas where the homes were huge, and it inspired me to shoot for my dreams.

After pleading with my parents to go where my neighborhood friends were headed, I attended my local high school. However, I discovered that peers sometimes go separate ways during this time. I tried to remain friends, but not everyone wanted to stay close. So, many of us opted for different people with similar interests. Most of the guys in our neighborhood didn't want to play basketball all the time like Johnnie and I. So I had to connect with the ball players, but now I'm just a freshman, and these guys were bigger, faster, and stronger. So, what I was in middle school was neutralized at the high school level, and the school was just so much bigger, too.

I saw that popularity was the name of the game being played and I wanted in. But I wasn't an athlete yet and was not that cool or even very tall. I remember running for the position of council president and not getting voted in. I will not lie and say it didn't break my heart; it did. But all of these moments played a role in shaping me and also helping me see how it felt to be treated as less than others because you didn't seem to be enough. I think this is when I decided that when I made it big, I was going to still see others for who they were and show love. I think that's what we all were in search of.

Many people lose themselves in school trying to impress the wrong teammates. They develop unbecoming habits and play roles to get attention and gain acceptance. Many youth raised to be respectful, turn and become people they are not, just to fit into the wrong crowd. The thing is, life has rules, just like the court, and before long, they begin catching fouls and missing opportunities.

Nowadays, when I speak in schools, I aim to promote the role we are supposed to play. That is to be a student and accept instructions from our academic coaches. Just like an athlete, you play the role of a student in the game, learning from your coaches. I played my roles as a student and an athlete during high school. I became a solid player and did my best on the court. I thought college recruiters would notice me despite being a leading scorer. No coaches seemed interested in my abilities. I did not have a big body or the height to make me stand out, but I worked on my game to make up for it. I could have been discouraged—and, at times, I was. However, I vowed to stay resilient, build my skills, and play my best.

# *"Somehow, I felt like I was still going to be a champion."*

I was once told that everyone loves a winner, but I found that people have preferences, and there are specific types of winners they prefer. I wasn't the right type. Some people held popularity or flaunted having parents with money and power. I represented myself, and most of my peers were not drawn to me. I was not the cool kid in school. I was a quirky guy with some basketball skills. Nowadays, young athletes have AAU leagues and social media profiles to grow their awareness beyond the walls of their schools. But, back in the 1980's and 90's, we did not have the same tools. But I did have hope that I would one day become that guy on campus.

I wanted to finish high school like I was the man, and I felt that I could go out on top with a pretty prom date. However, this big moment taught me another lesson. My date stood me up. I asked, and she shocked me by saying yes. This young lady was one of those popular people with looks that caught everyone's attention. She attended a different school, and I knew I would be the man when I entered my prom with her. Maybe she noticed I was a good ball player and thought, why not? I wasn't as smooth off of it, which might have inspired what happened next.

I called her on the evening of my prom, but she didn't pick up. I think I knew she wasn't coming, but I wanted to assume her parents were dropping her off. This was a time when teenagers didn't have their own cell phones. So, I waited and waited. Part of me suspected she had changed her mind. I was hopeful and looking forward to walking into the stares of my peers. But I realized she wasn't coming and had a choice to make. Was I going to allow another person to stop my party? Do I love myself enough to stand tall and go to the prom alone? I wouldn't wish this on anyone, but I would suggest to anybody faced with this dilemma to do what I did...Just go!

I arrived in a nice tuxedo and took my prom picture, which still sits in a frame between my two brothers, pictured with their dates. That day meant a lot to me, and I stood up like it was a game. I felt terrible but chose to push past my emotions and worry about what others might say about me. I am glad I did because, looking back and laughing at it now, the real test was for me to accept myself and display self-love. This was the test, and I passed it when it mattered most. I hopped into my parents' Alfa Romero and thought to myself, the beautiful butterfly missed her ride.

*"Tough times don't make the man; they just reveal if he has become one."*

# My Mission:

During this chapter of my life, I had to determine what I wanted and learn how to play the roles expected of me that would move me into a position to accomplish my big dream.

# My Methods:

The steps that I took that worked best for me were to work from the values and character that I had been taught early on. I realized that the clock was always ticking down and I only had a short window to use what I had learned to move on to the next level and that I had to get up over and over again after failing.

# My Measurables:

I walked away from school with my high school diploma and lots of teachers who would be willing to write letters of reference for me as a good student and person. And, I found out just how valuable self-love and self-belief were going to be.

# My 3<sup>rd</sup> Role: Pay to Play

*"If you want to get paid, begin by paying attention. Attention is a tool for building value others will pay you for possessing."*

My years at junior college introduced me to the role of personal accountability and team leadership. I grew into a body that would open some doors during this time. But nothing was handed to me, and there was a high price to pay. I did not envision having to pay to go to college as a part of reaching my NBA dream. I had trained hard and even led my high school team, but that didn't help me secure a scholarship.

I believe that during my final season in high school, college coaches felt I was still undersized for my position at six foot two. I admit I wasn't the biggest guy and didn't stand out in the room as I do now. So, I was not fortunate enough to be considered a scholarship-worthy player. But, I had many accomplishments on the court, and it was hard to understand why.

One explanation was that I was a ball player from the suburbs during the early 90's. These players were considered soft and not tough enough to play at the Division 1 level. It was assumed that the urban youth played aggressively because they had more to gain by using basketball to escape challenging circumstances. This is where organizations like AAU and the Junior NBA have leveled the field by generating more exposure for all youth. But, all I had was a variety of streetball courts to choose from that determined the level of competition I would encounter. And that is where I began making a name for myself. But, I had no clue about the risk-to-reward game of recruiting the best talent. The coaches and recruiters were looking for players that fit within their system. While most young ballplayers tried to be like Mike, the scouts sought a solid ROLE player. I was guilty of this as well, as I focused on displaying an all-around game. I didn't know what I didn't know.

## *"Often, a player's greatest opponent is lack of preparation."*

So, even though I was the size of a typical college guard, I was asked to play a forward or center role because I was one of the tallest players on my team. These are factors that no longer limit talented players. It's not uncommon to see the tallest player on a team playing the point guard position and shooting three-point shots. Back then, that was not what coaches were allowing at all. Your teammates would often determine the position you were made to play. I was not allowed to truly display how much my game was improving. But, speaking of tall, I had grown five inches since my final high school game and another inch before stepping onto the college court. I had to keep pushing and digging within myself to find that version of me that could make my dream a reality.

I followed my brother Johnnie, who had already joined the local Junior College. He had worked to pay for his tuition while also playing on their basketball team. So, I enrolled at the same campus, pursued the same degree, and worked at the same company. He had discovered that Roberts Oxygen had a tuition reimbursement benefit. That served as his scholarship, and after securing my job beside him, the company helped cover fifty percent of my tuition as a part-time employee. He played on the team the year before I arrived. At the oxygen plant, we got to work in exchange for tuition reimbursement. This opportunity kept us on our toes as we had to pass each course to be reimbursed.

You should be careful who you follow and what you copy from them. As for me, I knew that I couldn't go wrong with following the example of my father and older brother. Both of them had proven consistent and intentional with their decisions and roles. However, there was one significant choice that I copied from Johnnie that almost cost me my dream. In his final year of high school, Johnnie suffered a severe elbow injury that affected him. The reason why his high school career ended abruptly was because his varsity coach made some insensitive ethnic comments in the locker room during halftime. So my brother removed his team uniform, handed it to an assistant coach, and exited the locker room to watch the 2nd half from the stands. This meant he wouldn't have the chance to play nor display his skill or incredible athleticism in front of any college coaches. He may have missed his shot, but he scored major points for not following behind an adult lacking character. Since junior college did not require that he take an SAT or ACT exam for entry, he chose not to take it.

When I saw that the college scouts had not recognized my potential, I headed to Junior College. My brother did not tell me not to take the exams, but I saw no need since they weren't an entry requirement.

## "*I do not recommend students skipping their SAT exams.*"

I registered at Montgomery College and immediately began preparing for the basketball tryouts. I was eager to figure out my role on the team. It was not going to be a breeze getting onto the squad. I heard that the coach had spoken to my high school coach, and he was told that I was an above-average player. The assumption was that I might still be an undersized collegiate player. But they hadn't seen me since my six-inch growth spurt, nor had they seen me get loose on the court.

I was relentless, and that was like my superpower. And this was an opportunity I was going to leverage. I had nothing to lose and everything to gain. But, to lead this team, I had to convince the coach and the returning players. Coach Hobson was a tall, slender man with a fiery personality and an incredible passion for the game. He had been a ball player, so I figured he would know a good player when he saw one. He had many expectations for his players, and I can tell you that he was a difficult coach to impress. I knew that I had to be exceptional if I wanted to lead his team.

I trained hard to improve and perfect my skills so that when I had the chance to play, there would be no question about my ability. Keep in mind that there were already guys who had played for him the previous year and seemed to be the coach's favorites. However, I did not lose confidence in myself. It would be a tough battle, but I was prepared to try my best to earn a spot on the team. Weeks later, the tryouts finally began, and the competition was intense. We fought to make the team and played even harder to earn starting positions. When I succeeded, my next task was to win everybody over and become their leader. But first, I needed to gain all my teammates' respect and my coach's trust. The role that this moment played for me was to begin practicing ways to win others over. And I would have to learn to accomplish this while being viewed as their competitor.

We all wanted the same thing: the starring role. And I wanted to be our team leader. But how was I going to convince the guys to trust me? As I wrestled with walking the line, I began to recognize our team dynamics and some potential barriers to our winning. I slowly assumed the role of helping our team transition from competing to becoming teammates. I could see the coaches slowly begin to acknowledge when we worked well together and more and more.

Basketball helped cultivate my growth mindset and positive attitude, which were just the soft skills my coach was looking for in a leader. Despite being the skinny kid from the local high school, I made the team. I'm sure I was (initially) easy to underestimate. However, my miraculous growth spurt continued throughout my first year of college. I grew another inch to become six foot, nine inches tall. It was very unique to be such a late bloomer. But now I know that it all happened in divine timing. Had I grown earlier, I might've accepted a scholarship to a small university and never walked into what awaited me.

It wasn't just my height that went up. My confidence and skill level improved as well. You see, I had been shorter with a slim frame. My father had trained me to be a quicker player, making up for my lack of size and strength. I had developed agility and skills that offered me an edge over the taller and bigger players who were (often) slower than me. As I grew, I maintained my agility and now had the advantage. I was too tall for the short guys and too agile for the big ones. I started to dominate each game. My coaches and teammates became more confident with the ball in my hands, giving me more chances to run the team and the offense through me. When I played, there was no stopping me. Other players tried, but they couldn't match my energy. I was evolving into a star.

I was growing a local fanbase, and people showed more interest in me. Some began to come to watch my games and cheer us on. I even remember some of the guys at Robert's Oxygen began to take time to check out a game. Johnnie and I were still working as painters, hunching over oxygen tanks with stained overalls and painting away. We were playing our role. Although our tasks might've seemed meaningless, our work made the hundreds of rented tanks look new. The clients of Robert's Oxygen always had freshly painted cylinders, which was a drastic improvement from the old rusty tanks that typically made up the marketplace.

At that time, I could not have imagined that we were building character and playing our role. Our job was sitting in that painting room and making all those cylinders look better. And we did it diligently as we knew it would serve a purpose along our journey. I leveraged Junior College to grow my skills and showcase myself to major university coaches. I just continued to play my role at the oxygen plant, in the classroom, and on the court as an investment in my future.

The attention started to come from everywhere. And I, Jerome Williams, the kid from the suburbs, was proving he was on top of his game. With each 27-point and 20-rebound game, I proved I was worthy of colleges expressing interest in me. However, even if I wanted to, I could not transfer since I hadn't taken my SAT exams. I would have to complete my two junior college years and graduate to move on. So, I had to remain dedicated to my role as a student-athlete and keep my grades above all B's to ensure I was ready for my next opportunity.

My father was still actively encouraging us to improve our game. When we were free during the weekends and on holidays, he would go with us to play streetball at different courts around Washington,

D.C. I was able to put my game to the test, improve my skills, and build more exposure beyond my suburban college campus. I played against so many talented players that each made an impression on my game as we tested each other. And at one of these courts, I'd meet my first unsung hero. He was a small guy with a big personality. He was a selfless man known to help ball players secure scholarships to play at more prominent colleges.

Coach D was like a basketball matchmaker who would arrange for players to meet coaches who might have overlooked them. Johnnie and I were getting to the point where the local courts didn't present the challenges that would help us continue to improve. And I needed to face off with more elite players to prepare for the next level.

Coach D would invite players with higher skill levels to play together in gyms he may have ~~rented~~ for us. And the way Johnnie and I stood out indicated to him that we were of a different breed and hungry for growth. So, he pulled our father aside and told him he could see our potential to become great players. But, we needed more exposure than playing in the suburbs. So, Coach D made one of the most important calls that changed my life and ushered in my second unsung hero.

He introduced us to Dr. Joe Carr, another short guy with a vortex of a personality. He was a sports psychologist who traveled worldwide, counseling his clients during the week. He would return by Sunday to open the doors to a private school gym in Washington, D.C. This gym was affectionately known as "Doc's Gym." It was like no gym I'd ever been in.

First and foremost, it was by invitation only. Doc had a rolodex filled with the numbers of all of the best players, and one by one, they would arrive to play. It was an honor to be welcomed into this private family. There were players from junior colleges like us, great players from top high schools, and even some guys who were home from playing professionally in other countries.

Dr. Carr arranged match-ups to help each player improve at their position. So, just like Coach D, he was keen on taking us out of our comfort zones by putting us against better players to push us. He would assign me different opponents depending on their skill sets and position. This helped to stretch my game and develop me into an elite point guard. At Doc's Gym, he kept the ball in my hand, allowing me to grow my confidence versus players awaiting me at the next level.

It was during those Sunday runs that I realized I could play at the highest level and be dominant and successful. But, there were no cameras at the gym, which sometimes made me worry that I might not connect with the big-name coaches. But they say, "Be careful what you wish for because you just might get it."

I would plan my group trip to Daytona Beach in Florida during spring break each year. My buddies would pay me to handle all the logistics for our room and travel. They didn't realize I would exclude myself from the overall price and let them know what everyone owed for the trip. This was my break away from college and the basketball season, and I looked forward to it. My parents would lend me their conversion van with reclining seats, TV, and VCR. I had to drive the entire 700 miles down and back, which is why I excluded myself from paying any of the travel expenses. My dad taught me to maintain my focus when driving long distances, and I always returned the van without a scratch.

I never forget that trip because fate caught up with me along the boardwalk. My best friend Kevin and I saw a crowd and heard music that drew us towards it. Coca-Cola was hosting a Dr. J autograph session. There were so many spring breakers surrounding him that we couldn't get close. But, as height would have it, I stood out amongst the crowd and got the shock of a lifetime. Dr. J stands up and uses the microphone to call me out of the crowd to play him one-on-one. The crowd went crazy before I even got to the makeshift court. They were in for a treat!

As the game began, we went back and forth, and the crowd got loader and loader. Shots, layups, and even dunks entertained a growing audience. I think Doc was surprised that I was ready for him (almost). With the game tied, the ball was in his hands, and the next point won. He jab-stepped, and I extended my hand to cut off the lane. He grabbed it, which locked me in position as he took flight and dunked the final basket. I was that little kid again, playing on his little hoop with the real Dr. J. We hugged, and as I turned to walk away, he said,

"I'll see you play in the NBA soon." I was blown away and in a daze for the remainder of my trip.

As I made my way back home, I returned to my routine and workouts. I remember playing with a different edge to my game, with Dr. J's words echoing in my head. Then, one Sunday, not long after my trip, we showed up to play, and guys from Georgetown University showed up at the gym. It was not just another Sunday because Coach John Thompson was in the building. This man was considered one of the best college coaches of all time.

He had come to watch his players play. These guys were–solid! However, they had nothing on me. I had grown as a player, and I was ready for them. The bigger players were a bit too slow to stay with me. So, when the smaller guards attempted to guard me, I was too tall and dominated them as well. My unique journey had given me an advantage in my development as a player. I was like a hybrid! I took over the court! It was my time to shine... Coach Thompson left before we finished playing, but that was an amazing day I'll never forget.

Early Monday morning, I was back in class, and then I went to my job at Roberts Oxygen to paint some more cylinders to help pay my tuition. That next Sunday, my life changed. I was told Coach Thompson was impressed; I even heard he was amazed. He kept coming back to watch me play. I knew this was going to lead me to my next chapter.

## My Mission:

During this chapter of my life, my role was to accept responsibility for covering my education beyond high school. I had to secure and sustain an income source to cover my academic expenses.

## My Methods:

The steps I took to excel during this critical part of my journey included becoming a relentless opportunist who leveraged everything. I focused on solidifying the habits of being Dedicated to my studies, Determined to meet the challenges before me, and Disciplined enough to keep improving my game.

## My Measurables:

I am most proud that I walked away from Montgomery College (Germantown) with an associate's degree and the grades to qualify for admission to Georgetown University. I was indeed a student-athlete.

# My 4ᵗʰ Role: The Right Answer

*"The Man who knows how will always have a job, the man who knows why will always be the boss."*

-John Thompson, Jr.

If I were a guy without dedication, determination, discipline, or a mindset to overcome dilemmas, I might have already fouled out of the game. And you would have never heard of my name.

Throughout my journey, opportunity often presented itself when least expected, but in my case, it found me on the court, and I was prepared to score my dream. Sometimes, it is the detour that leads to the destination. Tony Robbins is known for his famous quote, *"It is in moments of decision that destinies are shaped,"* and I couldn't agree more.

In the previous chapter, I mentioned that Coach Thompson would come to watch me play. His excitement continued to build to the point that he arranged to meet my family and talk about offering me a basketball scholarship. He discovered that I had not taken my SAT exam during our meeting. The disappointment was evident on his face. Not taking the exam would greatly challenge my entry to Georgetown University. If I had taken them, transferring my credits would have been much easier, but now, it would be a challenging process. He spelled out the steps I would need to follow to attend Georgetown. First, I would need to graduate from Junior College. The second requirement was that I would not get into Georgetown as a traditional athletic transfer. I would have to apply much like a conventional applicant and qualify under its rigorous selection process. Coach Thompson may have assumed I was out of position, but I wasn't. And. I was not going to let him walk away with my opportunity.

## "I graduate from Junior College next month."

He looked at me and said, "Yeah, but you have got to get into Georgetown with your grades now." Many student-athletes focus on playing the game so much that they forget about winning in the classroom. Coach Thompson must have assumed this about me and concluded that even though I was graduating, I may not have the grades to get accepted by Georgetown University admissions. Coach was ready to open my doors, but at this point, he was giving up on me and ready to walk away. And, thinking here was another talented player, he was willing to help but was out of position for the opportunity.

"Well, sir, I have all A's and B's, and I have also just won a student-athlete award for my excellent grades," I responded. I could tell he was surprised. A great athlete and student in one? Maybe he had not seen this combination very often, so he assumed my grades were average. He was impressed and ready to welcome me to the Hoya Family.

This is a dilemma I had not foreseen. I cannot say that I was dedicated to my books to get into Georgetown because I didn't even know it was coming. This was my reward for hard work and sacrifices to keep my dream alive. My efforts defeated my mistake and granted me access to Georgetown without an athletic pass. I got a scholarship as a student who could also play basketball.

## "Chance favors the prepared mind."
-Louis Pasteur

Some might say I got lucky, but luck didn't save me here. It was my dedication, determination, and discipline that did. When Coach Thompson saw me and identified my skills at Dr. Carr's Gym, I was a 6'9" point guard. Georgetown was known for having great centers and power forwards. John Thompson had a reputation for developing big men. He would slow the game and have guards pass it into the big guys. He was so good at this kind of system that he produced three NBA centers (Patrick Ewing, Alonzo Mourning, and Dikembe Mutombo).

Heading into Georgetown, I was recruited as a point guard, which was new for Coach. It would change their reputation as a -big-man type of school. It would have been great to be allowed to play that role. Honestly, I felt on top of the world! But shortly before the season started, I learned I would no longer be playing the point guard position. It just happened that Coach Thompson had received a call from Allen Iverson's mother before school resumed. She requested that her son be considered for a scholarship. When he agreed, Allen was assigned my role on the team. This shuffle would significantly change me as a player and how I was seen. It would also shift the trajectory of my career going forward.

Coach Thompson was aware of my flexibility, and because of this, he asked me to accept a different position that Georgetown needed me to play. I would be moved from playing a distributing role to a receiver. Playing as a power forward would see many of my strengths held back. I couldn't display my ability to dribble the ball down the court or display my dominant ability to score. It put me in a position where I had to wait for the ball to be passed to me, and that was tough, but I accepted the role of becoming a defender and rebounder.

However, I felt limited as a player. I was playing out of position and in a role that I had to adjust quickly. It is true that I was a great player and even flexible. But it was disheartening to take on a new role. I was finally out of Junior College, where only a few people came to see me play. Now, our games would be broadcast on live television. As any player hoping to make it to the NBA, this was the opportunity to showcase my skills and get noticed. Yet here I was, a scorer playing the role of a defender. I finally had the chance to show the basketball world what I could do, but it felt like my laces were tied together, and my hands were behind my back.

I could have been angry at the coach for altering my role, but where would that get me in my career? I found myself facing yet another dilemma. How do I keep my mind in the right place?

How do I keep my attitude positive and play my game?

I had a choice: I could let this challenge cost me my dream of making the NBA or make this situation work for me. It required me to change my mindset, adjust my attitude, and alter my perspective. I had to ask myself, what do I need to do to play this role in the best way possible and make an impact on this team?

One thing was, and always has been true: I am not a quitter. And there was no way I was going to give up. I would take what was given to me and make the most of it.

## *"I was a relentless opportunist willing to leverage everything."*

I can remember the day Allen and I first met. There was much hype around his name, but I had yet to learn who he was without the internet or cell phones to look him up. When I met him, we were both in the gym, and I was looking for a bigger and taller guy.

I remember asking him for help identifying which guy in the gym he was. So, I said, "Hey, I'm looking for this guy named Allen Iverson. You know which one is him?"

He instantly replied, "That's me." I was shocked! Everything I had heard about him was difficult to attach to his slender frame. I had heard about him dunking a ball from nearly the free-throw line and making big-time shots. He appeared to be under six feet tall. But I was about to find out how amazing a game-changer he was. My respect for smaller players was changed entirely after playing with Allen. We laced up together for two years. We were Big East champions during my senior year, while Allen was the player of the year in the Big East.

He was a class act and made many exciting plays in practice and games. It wasn't hard to see that he would be a great NBA player.

The one thing Coach Thompson constantly talked to me about had nothing to do with basketball. He would often speak about life in general and handling our business. I'll never forget when he shared one of the most potent quotes: ***"Those who know 'how' will always have a job, but those who know 'why' will always be the boss."*** I used to replay those words over and over again in my mind. It was like a riddle.

I was still learning how to play basketball. I never understood or couldn't grasp many of his words back then. I believe Coach was explaining and exposing these concepts so we would seek out the deeper meaning or the "why." Coach Thompson fueled everything moving forward. I was learning how to play the game of basketball, beyond the drills and past the plays, and how to play for pay. I was learning how to make basketball my profession, and that was one of the most invaluable lessons I learned at Georgetown.

I was playing in a conference with the best and most talented players. I had teammates who would also become professionals, and there were some very skilled guys who, for one reason or another, did not make it, such as Victor Page. Coach Thompson was always teaching from his quote - 'Those who know 'how' will always have a job." So, he was also trying to give us an insight as to how money circulated on the big stage. His lessons as to "why" centered around the owners of the NBA, the television networks, and product brands.

On one occasion, Coach Thompson sat us down, and everybody wanted him to give a long speech. This would limit the time we had to run during practice. On that particular day, he gave us the big picture. He had an envelope in his hand that he had just received from Nike. The envelope consisted of a statement with his quarterly earnings.

He was on their board of directors and received a letter about a recently attended meeting. He showed us the check that accompanied the letter, passing it around so everybody could see it. It was over a hundred thousand dollars. I couldn't fathom how he was getting that amount of money, but it was simple. The top shoe companies were beginning to endorse high-profile college coaches.

That's when it clicked for me. I also needed to figure out "why" he was chosen and "how" I could be.

# "I promised myself that I would never be the dumb jock."

To summarize, Coach Thompson's teaching style put it all together for me. I may have never learned how to accept and thrive within my role without him. He helped my teammates and me see the purpose and power of completing our university experience with degrees in hand, and that's why I feel he was a game-changer.

So, good things began to happen because I accepted (and did not reject) my new role as a defender and rebounder. At the end of my junior year, I was invited to USA Basketball tryouts in Colorado Springs. This was that opportunity to showcase my skills and collect Team USA gear. This was the camp where all the top college or high school players were invited to play on the USA team. It was a competition to find the best players in the country. The sole purpose of this elite camp was to determine whether the players involved had what it takes to play at that level.

The entire point of the USA basketball trials was to see how well we performed under scrutiny and pressure. They had the best coaches observing our every move, with top talent guarding us and the most ruthless scoring system. The top players were there, and some became future NBA players like Tim Duncan, Allen Iverson, Marcus Camby, Kerry Kittles, Ray Allen, John Wallace and Charles O'Bannon.

Some future Hall of Famers were all there; I was considered a newcomer because my playing resume included a lot of streetball and Hoop It Up 3 on 3 tournaments. For me, it was like Christmas. I had been waiting for this since the day I got their letter. I wanted to show them what I was capable of.

When I arrived at camp, I had one thought: to dominate to the best of my ability. The only person I was competing against was myself. I didn't care how good the other guys were, and seeing as these were the best players in the whole country, that's saying something. Training continued till the sun went down, after which I would eat and sleep. We were all being challenged to work through our weak areas. Everyone was competing for a role on the team. We trained under a microscope, and I remember asking myself how badly I wanted my dream.

I began to see that my endurance was my strength. It didn't necessarily show up during the one-on-one battles, but it did when we were playing full court. The fun part for me was playing with future NBA all-stars.

After four days of tryouts, drills, practice, scrimmages, and games, I returned to Georgetown, assuming I didn't make the team over such big-name players. I got a letter in the mail titled 'USA Basketball. The letter's first line said, dear Jerome Williams, Georgetown University:

# *"Congratulations, you've been selected."*

I was selected for the 1995 World Games for Team USA. My selection placed me amongst an elite class of upper-echelon players, but this fantastic opportunity created a dilemma for me. Coach Thompson called me into his office. He said, "Hey, we're proud of you for making the team. We're sure your parents will be excited. The world championship games are scheduled for this summer in Japan." My heart dropped.

It was an excellent opportunity, but what would I do about my courses? I hadn't expected to make the team – I must have underestimated myself. This is why I made plans to take three courses in the summer. As part of Team USA, I was expected to travel and play 2-3 weeks that summer. And I could not complete both, so I had to choose the right answer. If I didn't take the courses right then, I wouldn't graduate on time and put off the work till the following year. This would make it more challenging for me to accomplish my personal goal. Through dedication, hard work, and resilience, I altered the odds against me, and I was able to leverage my decision and position myself for future success.

My dilemma was: do I stay and take the summer courses as scheduled, graduate on time, or run with this opportunity to play for Team USA? I felt the exposure might get some NBA scouts to consider drafting me. I had been a responsible student-athlete to get this far. But this opportunity to represent our country challenged me and my priorities. To accept it would be like me placing athlete first and student second. So, I knew what I needed to do.

My decision would shock the entire basketball community. I chose to forego the chance to play in the World Games and instead took my courses as scheduled. Most people thought I was crazy to forfeit being on that team. They said it was a once-in-a-lifetime opportunity, and I should have grabbed it. However, it wasn't what everyone thought that mattered. What I saw as an opportunity of a lifetime was to graduate from Georgetown University. I was okay with my decision and quickly felt that I had made a choice that had long-term benefits. Choosing what would position me long-term now affords me options I still benefit from. If I did not graduate, I would be another guy in the NBA who didn't graduate despite being an intelligent student. I didn't want to be that guy. And what if I didn't get drafted for whatever reason? I wasn't ready to gamble with my future yet—not when graduating from Georgetown was a guarantee. I feel that this move displayed so much about my character. I was truly committed to being exceptional on the court and in the classroom. But...

# *"I was so scared when my professor accused me of copying."*

When I took my last sociology exam, I aced. However, the professor felt that I was guilty of plagiarism. So, I re-took the test, and again, after acing, the same accusations were leveled at me. I had studied well for the test, and I was not shaken when it was recommended that I take an oral exam. With Coach Thompson standing behind me and promoting my character, I took an oral exam with the professor. And, to the surprise of no one but my professor, I scored an A (again).

There may have been an implicit bias towards athletes or my ability to think and express thoughts like I had. He had no idea who I was raised by nor who they had prepared me to be. The situation allowed me to display that I was disciplined, resilient, and committed to my role as a university student. By passing the exam, I served the role of challenging his perception.

The allegations were severe and could've resulted in me losing my scholarship and being expelled. So, you can imagine the pressure on me to be as mentally tough as I was physically. And the thoughts swirling in my head about not taking a direct path to my dream, only to confront an even greater challenger off the court. This is when I sit back and thank my parents for sacrificing for me to get that strong academic base that saved me and is why I could proceed onto my fantastic senior season. We had another great year, and Georgetown made it to the elite eight in the 1996 NCAA Tournament. We lost to Marcus Camby of UMASS (who was going to be my teammate on Team USA). A lot was swirling in my head after the final clock ticked down at the end of my college career. Shortly after the chaos of March Madness, I was invited to the NBA pre-draft camps. I still had schoolwork to complete. But I was not going to miss any more opportunities.

Coach Thompson suggested which of the three pre-draft combines I should attend. And since I had been in this environment before, I had an idea of how it would be and felt very confident. The camp I chose was the three-day Desert Classic.

This was the NBA's pro scout camp for seniors. The legendary player, John Lucas, was the coach of my combine team. He was a great coach and told me he had scouted me and thought I was a good player. He had a way of making the players feel at ease while playing for him. One of my famous teammates was Steve Nash, now in the Basketball Hall of Fame. He was a tremendous passer and playmaker. He could shoot the ball well and averaged almost 17 points a game. I worked well with him, and our chemistry was invigorating. I played so well that I was named the most valuable player. Imagine that I won the award over the future two-time NBA MVP Steve Nash. The buzz that this generated indicated that my draft stock was rising. The accomplishment also granted me an invitation to the actual draft as a potential lottery pick.

But, first things first... I knew I had done it when I heard my name called along with hundreds of other 1996 graduates of Georgetown University. The faculty decided to acknowledge my academic excellence with their Raymond Medley student-athlete award. It meant that I had displayed excellence both on and off the court. What a way to end such an amazing chapter in my life. Those two years helped to align all the stars for my dream to come true. And what's the irony of being born at Georgetown University Hospital in May of 1973 and the same institution giving birth to my fabulous new life in May of 1996?

*"Trust in your abilities and always attempt to make the right decision for you, not the spectators in the stands of your life."*

# My Mission:

During this chapter of my life, my role was to represent my university and to position myself to win in life, whether that be on or off the court. The lesson this chapter presented to me was to believe in myself and the possibilities and to stand behind my tough decisions.

# My Methods:

The methods that allowed me to thrive and reach my two main goals were to remain disciplined enough to do what was hard every day, despite not having parents or coaches babysitting me in executing what was expected of me. I sought out the help I needed and accepted opportunities like student internships to ensure I would have a job after college.

# My Measurables:

During this chapter of my life, I discovered myself and wrote into my story another degree, an academic award, and an NBA draft invitation after being named the MVP of the pre-draft combine.

# My 5<sup>th</sup> Role: 1996 Draft

*"With the 26<sup>th</sup> pick in the 1996*
*NBA draft, the Detroit Pistons*
*select Jerome Williams."*

-David Stern, NBA Commissioner

I knew my life was about to change...

I figured I would be better off, having graduated from college, in case I did not make it into the NBA. Nevertheless, slipping to the 26<sup>th</sup> pick was one of those things that opened my eyes to the business of basketball. I learned how everything was connected to and with something or someone else. The school you attend, the players you play with, and the skillsets you have or have been able to display. They're all related to your personal brand and marketability. And these things collectively propelled me throughout my career and netted the most amazing experience.

But there's a story within this story of me being drafted, from what many have said, which was the deepest draft class in NBA history. As I returned from the pre-draft combine, I knew I would need a sports agent. Coach Thompson suggested I hire his personal lawyer, David Falk. He was Michael Jordan's agent and represented three Georgetown alumni. David came to my home and spoke with my entire family. Imagine a man in your living room who had been listed among the "100 Most Powerful People in Sports" from 1990 until 2001 by the Sporting News.

After conversing with my parents, I decided to hire him., but 48 hours later, I had a change of heart and decided that I didn't want to be represented by Mr. Falk. I then announced that he was not going to be my agent. Well, that decision was very impactful to my draft position and maybe my earning potential. In the world of pro sports, timing and leverage are critical heading into negotiations. Having an agent with multiple franchise players could aid a rookie client in several ways. One is that the teams feel a bit more pressure to consider a rookie represented by a super-agent who holds the power to direct their star player to a different team in the future. Thus, some teams might gamble on a rookie to keep the agent of their star player happy. So, my choice placed me outside that bubble of leverage and unspoken power.

I felt my draft position was secure, and I'd be a lottery pick. And why shouldn't I have felt that way? I had been selected for Team USA and had just earned MVP status at the draft combine. So, I opted to go with Lon Babby, a sports lawyer from William and Connely. They had just launched a new sports law division, and Grant Hill was one of their clients. My deciding factor was paying 4% of my NBA contract and 25% of all marketing deals. Or pay only the legal fees incurred during the negotiations of my contracts. On paper, I could see the short-term savings, and I had always been a saver. This is what drove my decision to change agents.

> *"I would find out that this move may have cost me much more than the benefit of saving some money."*

Finally, draft day had come, and the consequence of changing my mind about David Falk hit me right in the face. I ended up slipping over 13 draft spots to the 26th pick. Luckily for me, my sports lawyer represented the star player for the Detroit Pistons. Grant Hill was their star player, and he also suggested I consider hiring a sports lawyer. So, by some divine fate, I was heading to a team that never interviewed me because they felt I would have already been drafted well before their pick. The very thing that Falk had mentioned as leverage might have saved me from falling out of the first round.

I was the last player on TV in the draft room that night, which was stressful and embarrassing. But this is when all the moments that had challenged me before this one served their role in helping me keep my chin up. I think it was NBA champion Derrick Fisher who left me alone in the draft room when the Los Angeles Lakers called his name. My team was right there with me, and deep down, I knew I would be okay because I was a Georgetown University graduate with a job offer awaiting my decision. So, I remember sitting there thinking, worst-case scenario, I had a job offer worth $50k with one of the largest accounting firms, Authur Anderson.

# *"I was trying to wrap my mind around what was happening."*

Before the draft, I worked out for 22 out of 30 teams, which is quite a large number. In the interviews, you do a couple of hours of working out, and then you have lunch or dinner with the GM and a couple of coaches and scouts. I remember my first interview with the Boston Celtics. They had the seventh pick in the draft. Interestingly, we had ties with the Celtics because my coach, John Thompson, played for them back in his day. His coach would even watch me during Georgetown games and practices. However, they drafted Antoine Walker, who then had a stellar career. The Celtics were the first team I recall working out for.

Another great workout I had was with the Lakers. They had a later pick. They had thought of drafting me but ended up drafting Derrick Fischer. I was later told that it came down to a coin toss between our names, and they definitely won big time with him.

Allen Iverson, who was also my college roommate, got selected with the first pick, so he was already celebrating with his family and friends. But I was still in the draft waiting room, on live television, waiting to be selected. Nearly eleven players had selected Mr. Falk, and all had been drafted before me. This moment served an invaluable role in introducing me to the business of basketball and who had the power to make things happen.

There were two traditional routes that a player could take regarding representation: an agent or a sports lawyer. I had an idea of how agents handled business. They made decisions for players and literally told them what to do in almost all aspects of their lives. Players may not have been on board with it, but they were told that's best for business—and they would cite their experience and relationships within the basketball community.

In my opinion, too many players were used to being told what to do when it came to making big decisions for their lives and careers. I knew agents meant well, but that's not exactly what I was looking for or how I envisioned running my career and business. I wanted to be involved in every decision about my career and life, to be in control from day one. I needed a representative who would work for me and keep my goals in mind, so I chose to be represented by a sports lawyer.

> ## *"An invite to the NBA draft was a great opportunity for any player to experience it."*

I showed up wearing a tan suit my grandfather had gotten his tailor to make for me. Excited barely describes my feelings as I sat confidently beside my lawyer with my parents, brothers, and Uncle Oddie. Multiple teams had expressed interest in me, but I'd have to wait and see—and wait, and wait, and wait. The commissioner called out names and which team had picked them. I can tell you what it feels like sitting at the doorstep of your dream and awaiting someone to invite you in. You did all you could to get to this point, and now you must surrender to the process. So, I picked my chin up and awaited my name:

| 1. Philadelphia | Allen Iverson | Georgetown |
|---|---|---|
| 2. Toronto | Marcus Camby | Massachusetts |
| 3. Vancouver | Shareef Abdur-Rahim | California |
| 4. Milwaukee | Stephon Marbury | Georgia Tech |
| 5. Minnesota | Ray Allen | Connecticut |
| 6. Boston | Antoine Walker | Kentucky |
| 7. LA Clippers | Lorenzen Wright | Memphis |
| 8. New Jersey | Kerry Kittles | Villanova |
| 9. Dallas | Samaki Walker | Louisville |
| 10. Indiana | Erick Dampier | Mississippi State |
| 11. Golden St. | Todd Fuller | North Carolina State |
| 12. Cleveland | Vitaly Potapenko | Wright State |
| 13. Charlotte | Kobe Bryant | Lower Merion HS |
| 14. Sacramento | Predrag Stojakovic | Paok (Greece) |
| 15. Phoenix | Steve Nash | Santa Clara |
| 16. Charlotte | Tony Delk | Kentucky |
| 17. Portland | Jermaine O'Neal | Eau Claire HS |
| 18. New York | John Wallace | Syracuse |
| 19. New York | Walter McCarty | Kentucky |
| 20. Cleveland | Zydrunas Ilgauskas | Lithuania |
| 21. New York | Dontae Jones | Mississippi State |
| 22. Vancouver | Roy Rogers | Alabama |
| 23. Denver | Efthimios Rentzias | Paok (Greece) |
| 24. LA Lakers | Derek Fisher | Arkansas-Little Rock |
| 25. Utah | Martin Muursepp | BC Kalev Tallinn |
| 26. Detroit | Jerome Williams | Georgetown |
| 27. Orlando | Brian Evans | Indiana |
| 28. Atlanta | Priest Lauderdale | Peristeri (Greece) |
| 29. Chicago | Travis Knight | Connecticut |

My heart raced. Doubts started to creep in. I was losing my confidence. I even wondered if I had been wrong about my abilities and that no one saw me the way I saw myself. Why were they not picking me after all the tryouts and interviews? I had done well, and all those teams had expressed interest. Other players were picked one by one, eventually leaving me in the room.

I could feel my heart pounding in my ears. I had not been picked yet, and no one was in the room now. I remember feeling very low, but

I had not lost all hope. I remember that my lawyer was on the phone talking to the general manager of the Detroit Pistons. I was trying hard to stay calm but wasn't paying attention to what they were saying. When he hung up, he turned to me and gave me the news: the Pistons were getting ready to draft me with the 26th pick. "You are going to Detroit!" I beamed with joy. It wasn't exactly where I had thought I'd be heading, but I was grateful to be called into the NBA.

I got up from my seat, confidently walked to the draft stage, and greeted the NBA commissioner. Finally, my moment, the one I had been building up to all those years, the one my dreams revolved around, had come. I shook his hand firmly, smiled, and walked off stage and into the next chapter of my life. I will never forget that moment, and I will be forever grateful to the team of individuals who decided to select me.

I was heading to the Motor City and gave my older brother Johnnie that look. He knew that meant he was coming, too.

# My Mission:

During this chapter, I focused on making my first major business decision. I aimed to position myself as a top candidate for an NBA roster spot. I did all I felt would give general managers around the NBA a positive impression of me.

# My Methods:

To accomplish my mission, I showed up on time with a positive attitude. Many teams pushed me hard during my workouts and challenged me mentally during their interviews. However, I remembered to use the advice I had received from Coach Thompson and remained poised under pressure like Dr. Joe Carr had prepared me to be.

# My Measurables:

I can always look back and be proud of myself for reaching my dream and growing as a person as a result of the process. My mom was gifted the MVP jacket, and my dad saw his son cross the NBA stage, knowing his tireless efforts to teach me paid off.

# My 6<sup>th</sup> Role: Detroit Days

*"I remember being pulled into the basketball office and Pistons management telling me to get my attitude together."*

There was no time to waste. As a newly drafted NBA rookie, I had to be on my toes, ready to perform on basketball's biggest stage and under the bright lights. Needless to say, I was excited to begin. The day after the draft, I flew to Detroit to meet with my new coaches and practice with any players still in town.

There were staff assigned the role of assisting me in finding a place near the practice facility and teaching me to navigate my new city. I opted to rent a simple two-bedroom condo. It was a logical and money-saving strategy because I was not planning to indulge in an extravagant lifestyle. I didn't purchase a new vehicle; I kept my customized 1989 Chevy Blazer. I wanted nice things and a big house, too, but I had just been drafted number 26<sup>th</sup>, and that came with a $700k salary, not the millions I had envisioned. That's not bad compared to my initial job offer of $50k with the accounting firm.

I was determined to avoid unnecessary debt and prevent stress that might have impacted my performance on the court.. Johnnie would eventually join me in Detroit, making the two-bedroom condo an ideal choice. My thought was that he'd come and keep me company. But,

I'd soon come to benefit from his community engagement strategies. I did not know anyone in Detroit, so having a familiar face and some support around was a relief. Word got out about my frugal spending and budget practices, and GQ Magazine featured me in an article about players who were smart with their money. The focus was on me resisting the culture of trying to keep up with veterans who had secured multi-million dollar contracts. But I was good at being Jerome, which was great for my savings goals.

I couldn't wait to play against the greats like Michael Jordan, Shaq, and Dennis Rodman. I entered training camp ready to outwork whoever stepped onto the court, and then I quickly learned that it wasn't just about energy and hustle. Instead, the pace, the shot clock, the defense, and each player playing their role. I was met with the reality of basketball becoming my job. And that transition was a bit challenging for me to wrap my mind around. This was nothing like how I had imagined; this was a real business...the business of NBA basketball!

The reality of taking my designated seat on the bench during pre-season began stripping away at my passion and hunger to play. Everyone wanted the same thing, and playing time was limited. This business required more than being just another good player. It meant I would have to accept my role on a team where everyone was excellent. Talented players were sharing my position, and each of us was working hard to earn a starting role.

I began to understand the difference between getting drafted as a lottery pick, which meant you were one of the first 13 selected, and just being drafted. All of these factors greatly affected my chances of getting playing time. A lottery pick is a label given to draftees considered the next big thing. With this label and accomplishment, those rookies often got more playing time. On the other hand, those of us who were selected 14th or after might have a bit more to prove as we often fell into the 'wait and see' category. This was one of the reasons why my playing time was minimal. I had dropped to the 26th pick and had an idea of why. In my mind, I was one of the best players; however, slipping in the draft impacted my playing time. My sports lawyer understood all of this, and he explained that I needed to keep training, stay patient, and wait my turn. "It's how the business works', he said. I tried to conceal that I did not like these rookie restrictions, but I was still thrilled to be a part of the NBA family.

Slowly, I would come to understand my initial role with the Pistons, and I would replay my lawyers' voice telling me to stay committed and wait my turn. So, I chose to make the most of my time on the bench, and why wouldn't I? I was a relentless opportunist, leveraging everything offered to me. The last thirty seconds of a game, I'd take it. A young fan hoping just one of us (players) would stop and sign our autograph, I would stop. The community appearances became my game, as I had the energy to leverage, and my brother Johnnie knew just what to do with it. He began building my brand around the things that were just naturally me being me. How he did it was so smooth that I didn't recognize what he was doing.

Imagine someone highlighting you as your authentic self and then positioning you to go just be that to the delight of a growing number of "fans." Thats's right; my fan-friends came first because I wasn't on the court enough to generate fanfare. Johnnie began meeting with Pistons executives to discuss using me for the community requests other players showed less interest in doing. And it worked!!! The more I did, the more I displayed the range in my ability to engage fans beyond the court. So, it turns out it was all happening for my greater good and development. My brother kept me so busy that I had little time to sit and complain about not playing. We had appearances to attend with Pistons fans who were excited to meet one of the team's players.

During our games, I would cheer for my team, jump up and down along the sideline, bringing that energy and firing up the Pistons fans. I would run to meet my teammates every time out, giving high fives and even hugs. I think some of my veterans had to get used to my enthusiasm, as my celebrations might have seemed like it was a playoff game. That is when most guys got pumped up to win. But I was just being me and showing that love that my mom always expressed when I came off the court. Think about it; I had front-row floor seats to watch great players like Michael Jordan, and I was being paid to sit in it when I wasn't up cheering.

So, it wasn't hard to sit on the bench with that perspective leading my actions. However, I admit it got hard when the games ended, and I would watch film of the shots missed, the mistakes made, or where someone could have put forth more effort to avoid an easy basket. I could see where I might have impacted the game, maybe grabbing some extra rebounds or pressuring a guard a bit harder. I often felt like this right after our tough losses.

I was winning in the local community and was happy to start the Jerome Williams Rookie Basketball Camp and Mentor Program within the Brewster Wheeler Projects. Then came an opportunity to contribute a column titled 'Rookie Diary' in the weekend edition of the Detroit News and Free Press newspapers. I might not have been a star, but I was starting to leverage my position to inspire kids who looked up to me for guidance. I got to talk to them about the importance of embracing their education and express how mine had helped me become who I was.

As my first season was concluding and summer break was approaching, most of the players were heading back to their primary homes, traveling, filming commercials, planning to party, or preparing for the next season. But, before I was cleared for the summer, the Pistons organization wanted me to play in the NBA summer league. However, there was a carrot that caught my attention. One of my assistant coaches would oversee the team, and he pulled me aside to say, "I want you to play your game. We are going to put the ball in your hands and let you do what you do." I was confused about why my role as an energetic bench warmer was changing. Sometimes, people are watching you when you least expect it, and I think my coach recognized that my talents went above and beyond my role. I had been playing out of position all season, which means that I had played a role on the court that wasn't best suited for my size or skills. But, I had made Team USA playing out of position as well.

So what was the coach offering to me? I would have to wait until the first game to see, but by the second game, I sensed my scoring touch coming back. I felt comfortable playing with the ball in my hands as the six-nine point forward that I was. I know it had folks talking and scratching their heads about why the Pistons "energizer" was running the show. But Coach Alvin Gentry knew precisely what he was doing. Maybe because he had witnessed something greater in me during our team practices. He saw the veterans struggle to contain my offensive ability during team scrimmages, yet I was not to get the ball in games unless I grabbed a rebound. So he was leveraging his power and position to say, "Show 'em what you got, kid." So, in the game against the Phoenix Suns, I scored 42 points and dropped 4 out of 5 three-pointers. I felt redeemed and renewed that, finally, I may get back to the role best suited for me. This was the same role coach John Lucas gave me during the NBA combine, which resulted in me being acknowledged as the MVP. I think that was also in the city of Phoenix. Maybe it was something about the desert climate, or perhaps that was just who I was as a player. But a player that many would never see in this role.

The next day, with plenty of games left, I was flown back to Detroit and allowed to begin my summer vacation. My brother Johnnie, who was always with me, suggested we immediately get back to training and further refine my offensive weapons. But, somehow, I knew that that wouldn't be a role I would be given. So, he decided to help me dominate off the court. And I can remember he would often say, "I'm going to build you into the Michael Jordan of Community Service." Over the next couple of seasons in Detroit, he positioned me as a celebrity activist who cared for kids at the deepest of levels. He focused more on my role off the court, which he felt would make me relevant for the other twenty-one hours each day. As for the three hours making up a typical NBA game, we had to wait and see what the coaches would allow me to do. But, we focused on what we could control.

For the most part, I never let my emotions affect my attitude towards my teammates or any of the coaches. I learned to hide that energy behind a smile or high-five. I would often affirm and reassure myself that I was Jerome Wiliams and was signed to the Pistons because I was worthy and had earned it. Without me recognizing it, Johnnie would arrange different ways for me to give back. But he was also creating a fan base that had nothing to do with me scoring points or collecting rebounds. When I would show up at local events, they began to show their appreciation for me. You could say I was becoming an influencer years before the internet would support these types of connections.

After a while, I even had some veteran players making suggestions for the coach to allocate me some playing time. That meant the world to me as I tried to maintain my confidence; not seeing the floor was challenging. But when Doug Collins gave me a few minutes to play, I left an impression for everyone to see. I had one gear, which was all out and a display of my relentless effort. These were my moments to introduce Jerome Williams to the NBA, and I made the most of every opportunity.

After one of my energetic displays of passion on the court, Rick Mahorn and Grant Long nicknamed me "The Junkyard Dog." They felt like when the coach would unleash me from the bench, I played like I was guarding the yard. And, as I ran around, creating havoc on the court, they felt inspired to nickname me. So now Johnnie and I were ready to rock and roll with my name, image, and likeness. This was the beginning of NIL for me, and even though I could still beat the internet down the court in dial-up mode, we were onto something.

*"Now imagine you're a kid at a Washington Bullets game, and you get to meet the Bad Boy Rick Mahorn, who smiles at you and tells you to work on your game. Then, about 13 years later, he welcomes you to the Detroit Pistons and gives you one of the greatest nicknames."*

From those initial opportunities, I started to get more and more minutes of playing time. And you know I took full advantage of each opportunity to make an impact. Soon enough, I had begun to grow a fanbase called the DogGPound. I also started seeing placards and homemade posters with my nickname in the crowd. I even heard people starting to bark as George Clinton's Atomic Dog would play after I did something exciting. The Junk Yard Dog became a household name amongst Pistons fans.

So get this... We decided to introduce my very own JYD mascot to enhance and promote my brand. My mascot was busy on game days, taking pictures with fans as they entered the arena. JYD also visited schools and hospitals with Johnnie while I was away. Now, imagine that your brand is growing even in your absence. It was really cool to arrive with that extra fluffy companion that helped me engage even more NBA fans.

I could feel all the love and support for this kid from Washington, DC. There was no turning back now. It was onward and upwards! I went from playing for a few minutes to getting a solid twenty-four minutes per game. But, just as I had begun getting used to my new role as a reserve coming off the bench to spark my team, I received the call most players dread.

## My Mission:

My mission was to carve out a role as a solid contributor to the Detroit Pistons. I also wanted to serve as a role model to young students with dreams as big as mine and offer them tangible ways to achieve them.

## My Methods:

I learned from my mentor, Rick Mahorn, to always be early to practice, seek out the little things others were unwilling to do, and leverage those opportunities as my building blocks.

## My Measurables:

I had a successful stint with the Pistons and departed with a high value and a branded name. I had made a difference within the local community and won the NBA community service award. I earned a second contract there, making me an official millionaire. The NBA also recognized the value of my community image and invited me to join Dikembe Mutombo in launching its first Basketball Without Borders in Africa.

# My 7th Role: Toronto Trade

*"If I was going to be the first player at practice, I needed to hop in my truck and drive overnight to Toronto.*

In Toronto, I had to figure out my new role on and off the court. I played with Charles Oakley and Antonio Davis, two great power forwards in the game. I knew I could learn a lot from them. So, it turns out that I would continue my role as the six-man coming off the bench. But off the court, I was about to become a champion in the provinces making up Canada.

I had established my dog Pound in Detroit. Now, I had to reestablish that same kind of fan relationship off the court in Toronto. But then it happened... I checked into the game the next day after being traded by the Pistons. I was the first to practice that morning, as Rick Mahorn would have expected me to do. I barely knew the offense, and here I was, checking into the game to assist Vince Carter and my new teammates. When I heard Herby, the Raptors announcer, add the Junk Yard Dog to my name, and the fans gave me a standing ovation, I was almost too emotional to play. This was the most fantastic debut of my career, and I knew it wouldn't be hard for us to connect with my fans up north.

I felt welcomed by their organization and fans, but I was curious how they knew of my brand and why they stood for me. Well, there's a story behind that, which I learned a bit later. Their response to me was tied to a few exciting things. First, the media had leaked information about me driving through a snowstorm to get there. This may not read as a big deal, but what makes this a unique case is that most players are given up to three days to report to a new team after being traded. This gives them a little time to plan their transition before flying out to meet their new team, either at home or on the road. So, the fact that I was sitting outside the Toronto Raptors practice facility before anyone else arrived the following day sent shockwaves through the organization, and someone shared that with the local media. This showed the fans that this American wanted to be in Canada and play hard for them. The second component that drove their applause was that they had seen my fire and energy when I played them as a Pistons player, and I think I had even scored some of my highest numbers compared to them. So, they felt they were getting an energetic scorer and rebounder who wanted to bring that to them. So that is what I planned to do...

> *"The DogGPound was about to become an international fan club, and I can hardly wait to tell you how it fell into place."*

On the court, I happily played the 6-man role for the Raptors, leading into my first summer of free agency after playing well in the NBA playoffs. I was able to help our team to a first-round defeat of the New York Knicks. It was a win that made franchise history and solidified my brand and me as a positive impact on the team. I remember asking the front office if I could purchase tickets for thousands of kids in the community. They were receptive to my request and gave me a block of seats in their gondola. This was an area in the upper deck of the arena.

I began distributing tickets in the community, inviting parents and young fans to come and watch our games. This gesture was met with a lot of enthusiasm. My brand grew in Toronto, and I got my first corporate endorsement. It came from the Indigo and Chapters

Book stores. This social marketing deal activated my name, image, and likeness to their youth book club. This deal aligned with many things I was doing in the community. It allowed me to promote the importance of literacy to my DogGPound fan club.

My role was to read books in local Indigo and Chapters bookstores each month. This felt like a Canadian continuation of my work with the NBA Read to Achieve initiative. I enjoyed how the deal was structured to impact the community positively and encouraged kids to embrace a culture of reading that would improve their lives. Upon Johnnie's arrival, we partnered with the Toronto District School Board to become the faces of their student breakfast program. My brother would visit schools each month and help arrange for me to attend the more significant events that might engage hundreds and sometimes thousands of young students. This was just a magical time in my NBA career.

So, heading into free agency, I had an opportunity to leverage my Bird Rights with the Toronto Raptors. Simply put, after several years of playing in the league, a player can sign a maximum contract spanning up to seven years with their current team. This positioned the Toronto Raptors to pay me more than any other team could, but my contract with them could not exceed seven (7) seasons.

> ## "I didn't know it would be my last NBA contract when I signed my deal with Toronto."

My negotiations with the Raptors began immediately after our season ended, which expressed their enthusiasm and interest. I was among some of their free agents, including Vince Carter, Antonio Davis, and Alvin Williams. Each of them was a starter on the team. The team began with my negotiations, which showed me how much value they attached to my role on and off the court. I had never sat in this seat, awaiting an organization to sell me on playing for them.

I remembered sitting in that NBA draft room, just hoping a team would pick me. Now, I was in the position to choose who I wanted to play for. But I loved playing for Toronto, and the fans and I were crazy about one another. So, I imagined they would come up with something enticing for me to consider. And, man, was I right! Before we even negotiated my contract, they started with endorsement deals for me. That's right; corporate partners of the Raptors had witnessed the growth of my popularity and expressed serious interest in it. So, my deal would also include endorsement deals with Coca-Cola, Sprite of Canada, Bank of Montreal, and other notable brands. These additional endorsements were already lined up for me and would come as additional exposure throughout the Canadian market.

Their presentation was just off the chain, to put it in Junk Yard Dog terms. They had designed a JYD logo with me standing with my hands up between the "J" and "D". That impressed me and even my wife. I felt like a franchise player just by the presentation itself. They showed footage of how I captivated the crowd and how the fans responded. I was shown the design plans for JYD Sprite machines to be placed across Canada. And, Sprite had commercials in mind that would air throughout the country.

It didn't stop there; I was also going to be the face of the Reebok franchise in North America, while in the United States, it was my college roommate, Allen Iverson. Things were turning out better than I had expected. There was more! My Reebok deal would come with my own JYD shoe, which I could design. Up until this point, I had only worn Nike since college because of Coach Thompson's relationship with them. My current deal with them was pretty standard. It provided me an annual stipend, plenty of basketball shoes, a credit for Nike gear, and about 500 T-shirts for basketball camps I might host.

This was a validating moment for all the times I had played the role(s) asked of me to the best of my ability, even if the assignment didn't allow me to display my actual ability. I felt like this was a victory for me to finally find a place that was excited about me just being myself and not somehow resentful that my brand, Johnnie and I financed with sweat, really connected with the people. I was thinking all this in my head while trying to take in all of this next-level respect. Then, they closed the deal by stating that I would be a starter for their team.

# "But, there was one more major component to this deal."

The Toronto Raptors included a Trade Kicker Clause as it was called. Any NBA player can get traded; however, if I were to get traded, I would receive a nice bonus for the inconvenience. That was huge for me because these were treats usually reserved for franchise players. It is critically important to know what it is you are looking for and "why." I had come from a stable and loving family, so when I had signed with the Pistons organization, I embraced the team and community like they were extensions of my family. So when I got traded in the way that I did and was informed by a media writer in another state that I had been traded and not by the team, it hurt me. But, it also taught me it's a business, and the show must go on.

I knew that by adding in the trade clause, the team was aiming to express that they wanted me in Canada, not just Toronto. I was being embraced by a country, much like an international football (soccer) player representing something much broader. I remember my sports lawyer calling me, saying that the NY Knicks offered me $10 million dollars more than the Raptors were willing to pay me. And I knew why! My name, image, and likeness had value, and there were parts of my game that team scouts knew they could unleash if needed. But most importantly, many teams knew that Jerome 'JYD' Willams would come in and play his role.

But, I was the general manager of my life, career, and family. So, I felt that this was an ideal situation for me and my family, which was beginning to grow with the birth of my daughter Gabrielle. And, because she was born in the Toronto Children's Hospital, she and her sister Giselle, who would arrive the very next season, both received Canadian and United States citizenship. So, even my kids got a dual citizenship deal that allows them to choose whichever of the two countries they wish to thrive.

I signed my Toronto Raptors deal for seven years and felt very good about it. I was ready to continue building upon my savings, adding to my investments, and further solidifying my greatest asset (name). It was not just my brand that was growing with each new endorsement. I remember coach Lenny Wilkins telling me my role had changed. He said, "I need you to shoot the ball more." The team wanted me to be more aggressive offensively. They were allowing me to be more creative and show more of my skills, which I was thrilled to do.

I wasn't given the point guard role, so the ball wasn't often in my hands, but I was averaging close to a double-double. This meant 9 points and often more than ten rebounds per game. At the same time, I was going full tilt in the community. The franchise backed my efforts 100% and needed me to continue inspiring young fans. Johnnie identified new ways for us to leverage the fact that we had an entire country to encourage to love basketball. But the Raptors knew our franchise would have to show them they cared about them. Toronto had just received the North American rights to market the franchise across Canada. This was huge!

Before this, they had been restricted to an area where they could market and promote themselves. The NBA does this to prevent teams from invading another's media markets. With the absence of the Vancouver Grizzlies, we had the entire country to ourselves. But Canadians were diehard hockey fans, and that was what the Raptors assigned me to work on. A big part of my role was to go all across the country, often with NBA Canada, to promote basketball and inspire more and more people to become Raptors fans (too). So, to track my social impact, my brother activated a 5-year initiative tabbed The JYD Project before social media became available.

We knew that all NBA teams were committed to community outreach, and we balanced my time between our programs and team efforts to give back. This was very important because Johnnie had built a system that was changing the game. I had already won the NBA community service award before leaving Detroit. I had a financial literacy workbook teaching teens about resume writing, banking, investing, and credit management. I had a youth motivation team led by my brother, visiting 3 to 5 schools a week to share my 3 D's (dedication, determination, and discipline) philosophy. I was even busy co-writing children's books with acclaimed author and literacy advocate Eric Walters.

The team was ecstatic over my efforts and all the local and national news it generated. But, what made us different was that I was able to activate my services during the season because I had my brother committed to helping me to inspire 500,000 youth to read more and aim for their dreams. We gave ourselves a timeline of five (5) years to do it. We also developed five (5) of our own youth programs while in Detroit to help us track our impact. This justified partnerships with the 4th largest school district in North America. The Toronto District School Board even provided Johnnie with his own office at their Student Success Foundation office, where they managed all their breakfast programs. Things were going great!

This had to be one of the peaks in my career as it relates to all that was going well for me at home, on the court, in the community, and in the boardrooms of my corporate partners. One of my memories during this time was a particular game against Tracy McGrady at home. I was dealing with some nagging ailments, but I knew I had to get out there and play because we had a lot of players injured. Vince Carter and Antonio Davis were out. I knew that the team was in a weak position, and they needed me to play well or like the old version of me.

I played, but it wasn't my best game. Tracy McGrady was out there having a field day. He was dunking all over the team, making these highlights, and taking advantage. I remember we lost, and it was just a bad day. However, my teammates and the coaching staff knew I wasn't in my best condition. They encouraged me. They said, "Don't worry about JYD. We'll see them down in Orlando in a couple of weeks." Yes, I would see them again, and this time, I would be a different version of myself. I went and circled that date on my calendar.

When we got to Orlando, Vince and Antonio were still not cleared to play. Before the game, the coach asked me to be a bit more offensive-minded because Vince was out, and I needed to play his role. I thought to myself, you all are offering me the Vince Carter "green light." The team depended on me to cover the points they normally expected from him. I knew I was ready to go and give it my all.

I remember getting the ball from Alvin Williams, and I got hot quickly. I mean, I was smoking hot. I was putting the shots up, and they were going in. I missed very few. My teammates were looking to give me the ball, and after I dunked a couple, it was open season. Tracy and I were going back and forth, and he was an all-star. I was given a shot to show them what I really was, just like in that short summer league visit back in Phoenix. I scored 30 points in that game and grabbed 13 rebounds to match my branded jersey number.

Our team won and vindicated the loss that we had in Toronto. All of Toronto was standing up, and they were very excited about that win. This was huge because Tracy McGrady had played as a star for Toronto before I arrived and chose to leave to play for another team. The city and the country took that personally. So it meant more than just another regular season win for JYD to lead the charge in getting that victory. From there, we made it to the playoffs again, winning 14 of our last 17 games in that season. I solidified my role as a starter. I even hit a couple of game-winners in that streak of 14 wins.

The franchise understood that I could play different roles at different times when needed, and I was happy to do so. However, I knew we were at our best with our franchise player, Vince Carter, playing his "Vincesanity" role.

## *"My greatest role was playing a supportive teammate."*

If there was ever a moment when a teammate needed locker room support, it was when Vince Carter decided to attend his college graduation at the University of North Carolina. Vince missed our morning shoot-around practice when he decided to participate in his graduation. He was catching a lot of criticism from the public and the media. As a college graduate from Georgetown, I knew there was nothing like your graduation, and you only get it once you've earned it. He had a huge decision to make, and I didn't want to make it any tougher, so I offered my support. What made the situation more hostile for Vince was the fact that we were in a game seven playoff elimination game versus the Philadelphia 76ers.

Most people would not truly understand what it takes for an elite athlete to graduate from college and still excel at their sport. It's like having two full-time jobs. So, I was proud of Vince for honoring his promise to his mother to complete his education. And, even though I knew he would have been a much stronger Vince Carter on the court had he not gone, I wanted that life moment for him even more. I will always stand in support of the tough choice he had to make to represent the concept of student-athlete. Looking back years later, with all of us being a bit older, you see the power in his decision and the message he sent to youth following his example of valuing education. I learned from all the amazing people I was able to work with during my time in Toronto. However, life has inspired me to enjoy the moments in the moment before things shift and change. And, before I knew it, the phone rang with that call again.

But, this time, it wasn't local media, nor was my coach or general manager on the phone. Imagine the respect of getting a call from the team owner asking you for your support in completing a trade that would only happen if I were included. The organization was in a dilemma, and I was the puzzle piece they had to let go of. I had so many great experiences in Canada, and as tough as it was to have to leave all of the support and love up north, I agreed to the trade.

And just like that, it was time to pack up, put the house on the market, and prepare to become a Chicago Bull. A big part of the process is attempting to remain professional when the moments demand that you honor the business of basketball. The one thing that will always stand out from that moment was when the owner and his wife offered to take care of our oldest daughter, who was in a premier private school. They knew my kids, and for them to offer that type of support will be forever appreciated. What happened was that one of my teammates decided that he no longer wanted to play in the city of Toronto and that he'd instead wish to go home to Chicago. It created a dilemma for the Raptors. They kept telling the Bulls management no. They tried offering other players, but the Bulls were adamant about including me in the trade. So, the JYD experience was needed in Chicago.

# My Mission:

During this chapter of my life, I focused on maintaining a work-life balance while my career exploded with new possibilities. My wife and I began our family, and I had to adjust to becoming a very popular dad.

# My Methods:

I had to learn along the way during this chapter of my career. For so much of my career, I could see many of the benefits and challenges coming and thus could best prepare for them. I had no way of seeing how I would be received across Canada, but I did notice that the organization and the community valued my values.

# My Measurables:

All my hard work and self-confidence netted me my own shoe and an award-winning national commercial with Sprite. I became a children's book author, registered actor, and celebrity.

# My 8<sup>th</sup> Role: Chicago Layover

*"It was a dream to lace up for the team that Jordan, Pippen, and Rodman had won championships."*

After I agreed to the trade to Chicago, a private plane was scheduled to pick us up. There was no overnight driving through any snow storms. I was older now, more refined, and less emotional about this aspect of the game. I took the time they offered to get my affairs in order. This was a five-player trade with Jalen Rose and Donyell Marshall, who left Chicago. The Toronto Raptors were sending me, Antonio Davis, and Chris Jeffries to the windy city.

Upon arriving in Chicago, I immediately met John Paxson, the Bulls' general manager. He sat me down and said, "Man, we are so happy we got you JYD because of all the community things we've seen you do and the roles you played for Detroit and Toronto. We knew you were going to be our guy."

He explained that they had two young players with great potential who needed to watch and learn from solid veterans who knew how the league worked. He was assigning me the role of teaching them how to thrive in the NBA. I was like, "Wow! That was a significant role. I was assigned to help guide and direct the future of an iconic franchise. I had never been asked so directly to become an influencer of young, talented players. But my vets like Rick Mahorn and Charles Oakley had prepared me to pass the wisdom, so I was ready!

Tyson Chandler and Eddy Curry were two of the most athletic players I had ever seen or played with. These young guys were unreal, and I knew they could become all-stars. I began my role by mentoring them and offering advice to best leverage their natural abilities. Their growth potential was off the charts. However, I knew skill alone was not everything it took to succeed in our league. They would need to embrace the discipline, commitment, and consistency of other great players. I made sure to teach what I was taught back in Detroit. For example, showing up three hours before practice and leaving two hours afterward. Not just hanging around the practice facility but ensuring you were seen putting in the extra effort to be great. My main goal was to make sure they caught that message from me if nothing else. I didn't know how long I would have with them, but I knew they would be fine if they just showed up like I had suggested.

Our trade took place mid-season, usually when teams get serious about making the playoffs. But my spirits were low, and my heart was still in Toronto. The one thing generating some excitement for me was the fact that Scottie Pippen was back with the Bulls.

## "Everybody knew Scottie could do so many different things."

He was one of my role models as a child. He had returned to the organization after spending time with the Portland Trail Blazers and the Houston Rockets. I grew up watching him play alongside Jordan and felt my game was like his. But only the players catching me in the off-season got a chance to see that version of my playing style. But Scottie had come to deliver perhaps my final lesson.

Observing him on the tail end of his career and seeing that his body wasn't holding up the same. Then, I realized that the great Hakeem Olajuwon offered me the same message in Toronto and Joe Dumars in Detroit. These were my examples of the backside of the game. I was beginning to see that time was ticking, and we each had to accept this game would end. Each of their transitions offered me a perspective that has proven itself invaluable. I told myself that I had better make the most of the moments and solidify a legacy to be proud of some twenty (20) years later.

Between all the games, the daily traffic, and getting my family settled, I hadn't activated anything within the community. Johnnie was still back in Toronto, fulfilling our five-year commitment to serve youth. So, I didn't have him with me to scout the city's needs or forge partnerships to leverage my influence as a Bull. I figured we would craft our strategy during the coming off-season. I knew I wanted to offer Chicago some of the things I had done in Detroit and Toronto. As for the court, I had a new head coach to get to know and trust.

This time, it was Scott Skiles, who was still playing when I was drafted back in 1996. Now, he was leading the Chicago Bulls. He was a hard-nosed, old-school type of coach. I was going to need to figure him out in order to serve my role in helping guide Eddy and Tyson. This is the master key that many players don't recognize, and then they eventually lose. By failing to identify the nuances driving your coach, you can actually work against yourself and invite an additional defender into your career. I have had to master this over and over again. From high school onward, I realized that many coaches were fixed-minded and had a vision for how they saw the game. And, unless you are a star player, you would be assigned a role to execute within their system.

My role was to learn both the strengths and weaknesses of my two young stars and encourage them to craft performance habits that would help them thrive within Coach Skiles's offense. Players and coaches often clash, and I have noticed that coaches are typically the winners of these locker-room battles. I've seen great players cut, traded, or their images destroyed in the media when they fail to comply with a coach. So, my initial advice to my guys was to keep the main thing- the main thing. I wanted them to protect their dream and remain professional at all times.

You must seek out the silver lining in situations requiring your time and commitment. Do not lead with your mouth, is what I was told as a child. Instead, assess the steps you will take and how your plans will grow to include more options and opportunities for you. Too many athletes make the emotional mistake of speaking from the alpha ego that sports have breaded into us. We often fail to fall back and follow the instructions. I've seen this mistake repeatedly, and it's like watching an all-star blow an open lay-up. It has cost so many great ball players the opportunity to display their talent.

I can remember that the situation was not as ideal as when I was with coach Lenny Wilkins. He was by far my favorite coach in the NBA for numerous reasons. But, the game of life is always about now, so I had to gain an understanding of what coach Skiles was trying to do and show respect towards him and his coaching style. When we sat down to talk, he made it clear that my role would change (again). This often happens in basketball, business, and relationships. I have found that managing my emotional energy allowed me to thrive better in whatever role I was assigned. And, often times I did not like it, but my coaches never knew that.

Instead of focusing on serving as a veteran mentor, he wanted me to play small forward, which meant that I would be going up against players like Tracy McGrady, Ron Artest, and other guys who were strong, agile, and very athletic. It was a significant change, and this meant I would be running around screens instead of setting them. I was not used to it, but Scott knew I was a vet in the NBA and that I could adjust. I scored more points and was still the 2nd leading rebounder on the team. This was just another opportunity for me to show more of my game. I shot more from the perimeter as a Bull than I had my entire career.

I was wired to do all I could to win on the court, but my responsibilities were growing off of it. I had a role as a parent that I had to fulfill and save time and energy for. Our oldest daughter, Sherae, had to transition to a new high school, so we were trying to support her. Imagine having friends in another country and then immediately transferring back to the States in the middle of the school year. That was probably tougher than my trade transition.

# *"The shot I knew I couldn't miss was being a great dad to my daughters. I had to win that game!"*

Our two younger daughters were still in Montessori, but they were learning the days of the week and started to understand the time. So they began to understand when Daddy would be away for one day, two days, or more. This is maybe the toughest role we play as athletes. I have rarely read or spoken with other players about how it feels to leave our families behind so often. Yes, we are able to provide them with a great life and the best schools, but we miss so much time with them over the course of our careers. My dad didn't miss a day, and I knew its impact. So, I knew the remaining years on my contract would probably be my last.

We battled for a playoff spot but fell short by one game. The season was over, and as it turned out, it was the end of my time with the Bulls. My moment in Chicago was like a short layover at O'Hare, and although my body felt like I was at the midway point of my career, I knew I couldn't keep putting my wife through this process. Later that summer, I got a call from my lawyer asking how I felt about a trade to New York.

# *"I thought, why not, and welcomed the opportunity."*

I played many games in Madison Square Garden during my college days at Georgetown. It was one of my favorite arenas to perform in. Here was an opportunity to play a role for the Knicks. I was disappointed that I hadn't served any youth in Chicago, but I knew my brother would figure out a way for us to impact the city, whether sooner or later.

# My Mission:

Before heading to Chicago, my mission was to determine what they needed from me and why they worked so hard to recruit me to the Bulls organization.

# My Methods:

The day I arrived, I sat with the team's general manager to discuss his expectations and clarify my role on the team. I continued to show up on time and serve as a veteran example within the locker room. I also sat with our head coach to clarify what he needed from me for our team to win.

# My Measurables:

My most measurable win during my time in Chicago was coming to a very profound realization. It made me stop to contemplate what the business of basketball was doing for my family and what it was doing to my family. This was a great point of reference that helped me win the game of life.

# My 9ᵗʰ Role: Guarding the Garden

*"I knew when we put you into the game that good things were going to happen."*

-Coach Lenny Wilkins

Now, I will be heading to New York for the next season with my teammate Jamal Crawford. I was excited to be teaming back up with coach Lenny Wilkins. The organization was headed by NBA Hall of Famer and former Detroit Pistons legend Isiah Thomas. I knew Isiah was aware of my days with the Pistons and my Dennis Rodman-type motor and defensive drive.

I felt that this might be an ideal place for my final chapter. I'm looking at our roster on paper and thinking we are going to create some serious match-up problems for other teams.

The deeper question would be, will everyone accept their role? We had Tim Thomas, Stephon Marbury, Allan Houston, Kurt Thomas, Penny Hardaway, Malik Rose, Mike Sweetney, Trevor Ariza, Jamal Crawford, Jermaine Jackson, Vin Baker, Jamison Brewer, Jackie Butler, Maurice Taylor, Bruno Sundov, Moochie Norris, and Nazr Mohammed. That was a super team with so much talent that our own egos could be the only defense that could possibly stop us.

Starting with myself, I had to accept that my teammate Malik Rose was already wearing my #13 jersey number. This was a number that not too many players wore, so I felt attached to it. I had just completed a half-season with the Bulls, where I had worn #11 because Kendall Gill was already wearing my jersey number. Upon entering the NBA, I had chosen that number to honor my parents, who were both born on the 13th of November and May. I can remember thinking that one of them should have stayed back at the hotel room as they cited my 26th pick and represented their birthdates added together.

The number meant something to Malik, so I reversed the digits and wore the #31. To me, this number meant completion or the end of a cycle. I also noticed that 7 months on the calendar comprised 31 days, and my faith aligns with the 7 days associated with creation. So that is the story behind each of the numbers I wore during my NBA career. As new seasons begin, all the players must attend a media day event to answer questions and help get the buzz going again for our fans. I walked into media day excited about the new season and to be joining the Knicks.

I felt like I was playing at home since I was back on the East Coast, where I grew up. New York was a place I would often visit to play some basketball. All the guys were speaking with different reporters from the press, and then boom! The staff asked me to take a seat on the media stage. But I was not wearing my Knicks gear.

I was in one of my Junk Yard Dog T-shirts. I felt compelled to let the room know that the dog pound was now in NYC, so I growled a little and barked right into the microphone. I wanted our sports writers to let the people know I planned to get fans barking in the Garden. I knew that would get everybody excited. My personality was designed for a place like the Big Apple, where folks could come and see the junkyard dog.

I could not walk down the street without my wife and I getting bombarded with dog barks and people expressing excitement to see me joining the Knicks. The community relations team already knew what they were getting and planned to introduce me around the city. They had me photographed with a pile of books in my hand to promote literacy. They were ready to launch their reading program, and I was already a published author with three children's books. I had co-authored books to engage reluctant readers with Eric Walters and my older brother. I could already sense it was about to be an exciting season in the community.

# "New York is one of those places that never forgets what you do for youth in the community."

My wife Nikk and I decided to look for a home near the team's practice facility in White Plains, New York, and register our daughters in school there. With our daughter Sherae entering her senior year and Gabrielle and Giselle entering Montessori, I hoped to make it through an entire season without any trade talks. As a dad, I did not want to keep disrupting their friendships and bonds with adult teachers.

We found a house to purchase in Rye Brook and quickly settled before the season started. Fortunately, and unfortunately, we had gotten good at this moving-in and packing-up thing. And now, it was time for me to begin getting into my mode for the season. But when thinking about our team roster and the fact that we had one seven-footer and seven guys standing between six-eight to six -ten. I felt like we were a Swiss army knife comprised of different variations of the same position. But, I knew coach Wilkins would lead us and make it all work.

I had no idea what my role would be on a team like this. We had four players that had been the face of their franchises. We had more than five no-nonsense forwards that were known for playing hard every game. We looked terrific on paper, but in reality, it was more like a powder keg filled with ego that you hoped did not ignite. And, just so you know, we had the highest salary cap in NBA history at 98 million dollars back in 2004.

The challenge presented to any team where so many of its players had already secured their big contracts was how driven they would be and whether they would play like they had something to prove or like they had arrived. I only had one gear, which was all out from pre-season to the end of the season. Whatever it was going to be, I planned to enjoy the ride. I was about to take to the biggest stage, playing with one of my childhood friends, Moochie Norris. We both had reached our dream of playing pro basketball from our weekend games at Docs gym years earlier. The coach had so many weapons to pick from that he began changing our starting lineup game by game to create match-up issues for our opponents. I was still waiting for someone from the organization to clarify my role. There were guys who could literally do each and everything that I was really good at. What made me unique was my *perspective, personality,* and *positive attitude.* That's not to say that my teammates did not possess those attributes; I just led with them on a daily basis. During my entire NBA career, my brother and I would focus on one main narrative: what can I contribute to our customers that makes me relevant beyond the court and after the season? That was a tricky question to answer as a rookie but not as a veteran.

I had been placed into different situations and around an array of coaches and players, and three words got me through and helped me thrive. My PERSPECTIVE allowed me to continue my career and not ruffle any feathers. My outgoing PERSONALITY amplified the Junk Yard Dog image that I was known throughout the league. My positive ATTITUDE helped me overcome many challenging situations and was the glue that held things together. I think that sometimes our team jerseys give the impression that all the players on a team get along, like each other, or even know one another.

We operate like any other business where everyone is hired to do a specific job or task. The organization only wins if everyone plays their role. This does not mean that the coffee room, just like our locker room, isn't toxic or that certain people don't like certain people. Like most Americans, we got paid a check every two weeks. So, I was that employee who showed up to work smiling, greeting folks, and helping management put out fires that might burn the building down. As the word of my core attributes circulated amongst general managers and coaches, it added to my trade value.

> *"What separates you from others who can do exactly what you do is how you do it."*
>
> Johnnie Williams III

That is it! My team was going to need a peacemaker. With so much talent and so many alphas sharing the court, sometimes tempers might flare. I remember a heated moment between a rookie and a veteran. The older player was not backing up, and this rookie was standing his ground. You never read about that iconic boxing match because I did not let it happen. Some guys felt we should step back and let them work it out. Maybe in the parking lot or at a park somewhere, but not on our team court, or in our locker room with press present to leak the details. This would give other teams the impression we were not together, or it could destroy a young player's entire career. So, I was the guy that coaches could count on to jump in and calm the situation down.

Training camp gave me the impression that I may have to patrol for signs of smoke rising between two or more players and spare my teammates and the organization any embarrassing headlines. This makes me remember a sideline situation that was about to go down during a game that would have justified its nickname, like the one in Detroit (after I was traded). But it never made headlines because I would not let that happen in front of the fans. I'm sure you're hoping I share some of the details of such an interesting moment in sports that never made it to the NBA history book.

So, imagine a team filled with scorers, all tasked with sharing one basketball. There were moments or stretches during games when players who used to be the first scoring did not touch the ball. This was the unique situation we were dealing with in New York. I remember coach Lenny Wilkins calling a timeout after reading the situation. He saw what the other team was running in an effort to stop us. During that timeout, he drew up a play for Kurt Thomas to get the ball inside. "Make sure we get it to him on the baseline," he instructed. Kurt was almost automatic from that spot on the court. But sometimes, Stephon Marbury would leave the huddle, run the play halfway, and then decide on an alternative option. Maybe one where he was taking the big shot instead.

Sometimes, it would work out; the crowd would cheer, and the coach would not say anything. But, when Kurt would come back to the huddle, I had to go into peacemaker mode. That called for me to stand in between them because I had Kurt talking about what he was about to do, and I had to say, "You know I can't let you do that." Especially not in front of all these Knicks fans at Madison Square Garden. I could see the press licking their chops and just waiting for it. They knew something was getting ready to happen. They just didn't know what. So, it was my role to ensure that you never read about that in the paper or saw anything crazy on the news.

A few plays later, a few passes Kurt's way for a few great shots, and the calm was restored, and cool heads prevailed. There were many moments like that, but never any altercations. This is not uncommon in team sports of any type. We are competitors, and at our level, we are supremely skilled and thus feel prepared to take any shot, maybe every shot. So, this type of stuff happens more often than not. The key is for teams to hold a roster spot for guys who keep things in the proper perspective. But they must possess the ideal personality to get along with everyone, and help spread a positive attitude. This type of role player is critical when things on the court aren't going well, or guys bring outside problems into the locker room.

I did play some basketball as well, with lots of rebounds and relentless defense. Exciting the crowd was something I loved doing, and I actually got the fans in the Garden to bark with me and at me at times. They showed so much appreciation for my effort and hustle on the court. We were out there having some fun. There were lots of no-look passes and high-scoring games. But I enjoyed watching Jamal Crawford do his thing and Allan Houston shoot the perfect jump shot. I had Stephon putting on a show every night, and Tim was the king of highlights. Then there was Kurt, "The THOMPyard Dog," and Malik Rose helping me hold down the paint. Trevor Ariza was slicing and dicing like a razor, and my main man, Moochie Norris, was like a master with a ball in his hand. It was a pleasure playing with Penny Hardaway, and I liked the way he changed the game. Maurice Taylor brought that Motor City muscle to the court. And my man Nazr Muhammed would pray for our opponents before punishing them in the paint.

We were rocking and rolling. My season in New York was an amazing ride that gifted me with so many great memories to share during my JYD public speaking experiences. I was able to play basketball and thrive in the most amazing media markets on the planet. My schedule remained filled with appearances to speak at corporate events and go deep within the community to talk with children. We had celebrities and hedge fund managers sitting in the front row at all of our games, and that made for some awesome networking. I knew I would only be on the court for a few more seasons before joining them in the stands. This NBA experience exposed me to many great people; some were running awesome companies, and others had some of the coolest jobs. These are just a few of the nuggets I plan to pass on to our youth.

Speaking of youth, some Knicks executives heading up community relations and partnerships witnessed my brother Johnnie motivate some students. He had flown in to provide our financial literacy presentation, and he had all the teens engaged and talking about managing life after high school. We had dinner, discussed our usual community plans, and he flew back to Toronto to speak. A few weeks later, I got a call from him saying that Knicks Community Relations sent him a contract to tour each borough making up the city, including schools in Connecticut and New Jersey. They wanted my brother to speak with young Knick fans about literacy and goals.

Imagine that Johnnie got his contract with an NBA team to be an activist in their city. But, get this: the contract stated that he had to fulfill all the speaking engagements even if I (Jerome Williams) was traded from the New York Knicks. This was major for a lot of reasons. So many family members would travel to assist and even stay with their brother or son during the NBA season. But there was this unspoken assumption that they were just cling-ons that generated very little value for the player or team. My brother was shattering that narrative, and every team I played for knew that this dude was different. Just the Knicks were smart enough to offer him a contract. The NBA league office allowed me to include him on all of my international trips to help support Basketball Without Borders, and together, we were proof of the NBA Cares.

*"I was looking forward to all that would come in the next season."*

## My Mission:

In this chapter of my career, my mission was to create a new career and explore the opportunities that a big city offers. However, in a busy city like New York, my focus was also on better managing a work-life balance because our young daughters were beginning to desire more connection.

## My Methods:

Establishing routines for starting my day, spending moments with the family, and mapping my travel time to avoid being late served me well. Creating my system was the best strategy for thriving through my opportunity.

## My Measurables:

We celebrated our daughter Sherae's graduation from high school, which required her to make many adjustments. She also had to overcome leaving her friends and existing outside her comfort zone. I was very proud of her for managing all of that successfully.

# My 10ᵗʰ Role: Early Retirement

*"Walking away from the game wasn't as difficult because I prepared for it. I had saved my money and had a solid brand to take into my post-career."*

I still had three years remaining in my contract, but I decided it was time to go. Well, it wasn't quite that simple. I was afforded a very unique opportunity that would allow me the choice to stay or to go. That said, I'll explain how I hit the lottery in the summer of 2005. Remember, on my entry into the NBA, I was not amongst the lottery picks, but my NBA exit felt like a winning ticket. I left with a solid name, a marketable brand, and the last three years of my NBA contract. Two future hall of famers inquired about me joining their teams prior to them both winning another two NBA titles between 2007-2014.

I had just played 79 out of the 82 games of my final season with the New York Knicks. Much media talk centered on the strained relationship between the NBA and its players union (NBPA), which I had served as a Vice President. There were threats about a strike, and both sides were talking tough. It was like watching a championship playoff series between two giants. The only problem was that both sides had to agree for us all to win; otherwise, the upcoming season, or maybe even our league, was at risk.

So, I'm thinking to myself, these guys are about to mess my money up, and all they've got to do is talk. I knew this because I had an open door to sit with the NBA Commissioner, David Stern, and the players' union president, Billy Hunter. Speaking to them individually, they said the same thing but sounded worlds apart in the media. Now, remember that I was playing for the NBA team with the highest payroll in NBA history at the time. We did not want a lockout jeopardizing our current contracts, so I did all I could to get an agreement.

Luckily, my daughter was finishing her last month of high school, so I was available to focus on resolving our differences. Now, here's a little history that most people never knew. There was a set day and time that the lockout would activate, and I felt like James Bond in a New York scene racing the clock. Well, I beat it, and the NBA lockout of 2005 was avoided. I was playing the role of mediator at that moment. And, if there was ever a point when my peers would need me to be a Relentless Opportunist Leveraging Everything, it was right then.

I had the direct numbers to both of the giants, and they both would accept my calls. Their secretaries loved me for always being kind and respectful towards them and never looking past them to get in for a meeting. This is important for you to catch the ball I'm tossing. I could only leverage the relationships I took the time to build. So, I built connections by attending all the meetings and making all the appearances they asked for. I could get to them, and they heard me when I spoke.

So, on the day that the NBA lockout was to be activated, I met directly with David Stern, and he realized the players wanted things similar to what he did. I remember rushing out of his office and calling Billy Hunter. I shouted, "Billy, I need you to hop in a cab and get to David's office. He's ready to talk now; we all want the same thing. Let's get this done!" He immediately traveled to the league office, and later that evening, ESPN reported there would be no NBA lockout. My money was safe... But., how does all that have anything to do with my retirement and me winning the lottery?

Well, it turned out that an amnesty clause was included in the new collective bargaining agreement that would allow teams like the New

York Knicks to waive a player on their payroll that was causing them to exceed the NBA cap of, let's say, fifty million. The Knicks were at ninety-eight million. When teams in more profitable markets exceed the NBA cap, a dollar-for-dollar penalty would be paid to the NBA. So, a team like the Knicks might have owed (in the neighborhood of) forty-eight million. That's a lot of extra cash, and it was designed to keep the league balanced and prevent super teams from emerging in dominant markets.

A couple of weeks later, I got that call from the team president and you know what usually happens when he calls me. So, he shares that the Knicks want to amnesty my contract. I'm thinking, what does that mean? He said we will waive you and your contract from our books. My mind went left for a quick moment, but he continued. "Jerome, this means you'll be paid your three remaining contract years just as if you are still with us, but for us to do this, you just cannot play for us this 2005/06 season."

Hold on...Jesus, grab the wheel as I wrap my mind around what is happening. Do you mean I will get paid for not playing? Not diving on the floor? Not taking all the physical abuse on my body? "Yes," he replied; "And I know that most of the teams in the league want a player like you, so you can maybe double your money." Thinking I can't wait to call my wife, I told him let me check with my boss and to fill out my retirement papers for the NBA. I don't think he expected my response; he knew from the very beginning that I was different. Walking away from the game wasn't as difficult because I prepared for it. I had saved my money and had a solid brand to take into my post-career.

My response and decision to walk away shocked many in the basketball community. Older veterans suggested I double down on the money I was making. But I knew my decision was the most impactful to some young baller trying to find his way onto an NBA roster that would need someone to leave the NBA so that he might enter it. Most people don't know that there is and was a set number of roster spots available, and most of them are already secured by players with multi-year contracts. I decided to leave in honor of something Rick Mahorn told me as a rookie back in Detroit. He told me to come in, make my money, and then move on so another guy could do the same.

It was just the right time. My two younger daughters were about to begin Kindergarten, and I didn't want to be gone all the time. Nor did I want to pull them in and out of school with team trades, as I had done two times with Sherae. My mind was full of all the new possibilities, and I was excited to get back to all the things I could not do while under an NBA contract. I left the NBA cold turkey and realized when the season began how much I would miss it. But my checks began coming every two weeks, and my girls coming out to greet me after school with million-dollar smiles got me through.

I was used to starting practice at ten every morning like clockwork. Remember, I would get to the gym three hours earlier, which means I would already be there at seven, completing my routine of lifting weights, stretching, and shooting drills before practice started. Now, I was practicing doing hair and packing lunches before hopping into Ms. Blue to take them to school. That was the name my girls gave to my custom blue Toyota Minivan that was the talk of the parent groups at their school. We pulled up with the music pumping JYD rap songs.

The hardest part of my day was filling the time they were in school. Our NBA schedules mimic a full school day as far as the timelines are concerned. Based on the time of day, it was like my body knew exactly what it was used to doing. I think this is why so many retired players begin playing golf. It offers competition, and it's played by many business-minded individuals. But most importantly, it takes up time. And that's what eats at a 32-year-old retiree. I had to literally practice breaking the habit of practicing and working out so much. That might sound funny, but I firmly believe that we are the sum of what our daily habits contribute to. My old habits justified an NBA contract for nine seasons. And my new habits would hopefully produce the fruit my parents were able too.

Now, I could drop the girls off at school, a role my wife had always played. I could say, "Daddy's got this," and start taking them to their activities and classes. Gabby had a full school day, and Giselle went for half. They loved riding in the big truck with the loud music and getting their booster seat dance on. We had a positive morning vibe, which was so enjoyable because I was with them. No more kisses goodbye, with them counting my days away and asking when I'd be home.

I would drop them off at school and head to the Madison Square Garden offices. I had a desk, a phone, and even a computer that I never turned on. My office was between the general manager's office and the director of basketball operations' office. Having an office at MSG was a big deal. It gave me a sense of status and pride. I guess it helped make me feel like I was earning my checks.

The way the Toronto Raptors had set up my final contract was to backload most of my money into the final three years. So, I'm at the office, having dropped off the girls and trying to look and stay busy enough to make sense of an almost half-million-dollar check every two weeks. Now, I don't share that to impress you but rather to impress upon you; this is what is possible in this country when you dream with action, effort, and a whole lot of self-belief.

I was educated in a public and then private school and received my degree from Georgetown University. I was stepping down as the vice president of the NBA Players' Union. I owned all the rights to my personal brand. I was an award-winning children's book author in Canada. My work within the community has taken me all around the world.

"This transition doesn't have to be so bad," I told myself. I knew I could do it. I couldn't resist that desire to compete and evoke the energy of thousands of fans. I knew I could sit in the seats as a fan and adjust to my new view, which wasn't nearly as nice as my floor seats on the team bench. I believed I could figure it out, and eventually I did. I started by meeting with MSG executives to assess what to do and what not to do. I knew the pen was in my hand, and I was writing this new chapter of my life into existence. The MSG team did not impose or put too much pressure on me.

Eventually, they asked me, "Jerome, what kind of ideas do you have?" I told them I wanted to produce my own TV show. It was a dream of mine, and I was excited to make it a reality. They liked my idea and said, "Okay. But do you have a production company?" At that point, I did not, but I had a reputation for getting things done. If I needed to have a production company, I was going to find or develop one. I told them I will.

So, I went out and hired a producer and a camera crew to help scale my ideas and put them in motion. I already had a concept in my head that I thought could work. It had all to do with cars. I wanted my show to focus on modifying different types of vehicles for NBA players and other famous stars. Think MTV's "Pimp My Ride" on steroids. I was constantly being approached by players asking me where I got certain modifications to my cars. They asked me what I wanted to call the show, and I said, "It's going be hot." Then it hit me, "Why don't we call it Make It Hot?" And sure enough, that became the show's name.

We had to figure out how to line up different celebrities and offer to make over their rides. I got with an MTV producer, and he agreed to start collaborating on ideas for the show. As luck would have it, he had just edited a video for this young up-and-coming star, Chris Brown. "Jerome, I should call his mom-manager and see if you can modify his new truck because he's getting ready to turn 16," He reached out and made the suggestion. She loved the idea and agreed to have Chris on the show. They were going to drop off a Ford Expedition for me to makeover.

I got on the phone with Chris, and he gave me some ideas of what he was looking for. We took his truck to my partner's garage and went to work to make it hot. This was an entirely new role, but I knew I would improve with practice. I visited Chris, and my camera crew caught me dancing with him. We played a little trick on Chris for his new song and video, "Run It." His choreographer taught me some dances to their new routine. And so, when Chris came in the studio, we made this skit saying, hey, let me show you I can dance. They had already rehearsed it with me, so I was prepared. When I came into retirement, I was open to trying things. It was new, and I liked it. I was having a lot of fun on my show, but at the same time, I was getting to play the role of a more present dad and husband.

I was still going to the New York Knicks games and practices. They still asked me if I had considered returning from retirement because they needed my skill and experience on the court. At the time, the Knicks were losing some games. Just being around, they felt like I could have helped them win. It had been my team, and I still felt attached. Having that winning mindset, I felt the urges pulling at me. I remember feeling like I could have given the team ten points and ten rebounds. This was why I didn't want to coach or remain in the front office. It was too close to the action, making it challenging (in my opinion) to move on with my life beyond basketball.

I knew I needed to stay away to remain focused on my TV show. The episode featuring Chris Brown aired, and it earned a point-six rating. It was an outstanding achievement, and our ratings continued to rise. It felt like an overnight success, with the telephone on my desk ringing off the hook.

> *"I was claiming another victory as an executive producer who could get it done; it felt terrific."*

I was genuinely proud of stepping beyond my comfort zone and playing an entirely new role. I felt proud that my first retirement risk was going well, even without prior experience. It proved something to me. I could do what I put my mind to.

However, I would soon be introduced to the complexities of TV. It became challenging, just like basketball. Decisions were to be made, and it all came down to my values. It soon hit home how tough it would be to remain on TV for a second season. My contract with MSG Network split any revenue from sponsorships 50/50. MSG had secured a sponsor willing to pay $2,000,000 for me to produce another six episodes of "Make it Hot". That was $1,000,000 out the gate in my hand, a great deal, or so I thought.

It would have been a massive win in terms of money. I would be getting a good return on my investment. I had purchased a lot of production equipment and remember asking my wife if it was something I should do. It was a gamble, and I had no experience. I was figuring things out on the go. I was banking on my intangibles, like hard work and my ability to learn new things, and I also had so many great relationships to leverage. However, my greatest challenge was me versus my brand values and principles.

The sponsor appeared excited that they would reap the benefits of their investment. However, the sponsor was trying to use my show to promote alcohol and tobacco products. My fanbase was the youth, and now I would be on the air, promoting something different. I was the face of my show and responsible for what I promoted to them, which was different from what my brand represented.

To do this and keep my show on the air, I would have to step outside my role as a role model. As a dad and community advocate promoting youth doing the right thing, I couldn't promote something that would tear them down. That wasn't going to happen. I decided to forego the second season to "Make it Hot " and move in a different direction.

Was it a big sacrifice? Financially, yes. However, sacrificing my values and integrity within the community would have been the greatest sacrifice. I did my math, and the opportunity cost informed me to decide on the community I supported. If I were placed in the same opportunity again today, I would still choose the community and remain true to my values. I firmly believe that life was testing me then to see if I would abandon what had gotten me so far.

During this time, I was considering my next move after letting go of my TV production. One of the things that I remember thinking about was becoming an NBA Global Ambassador because that was something that they were pitching to me. I had already worked with the NBA and Basketball Without Borders initiative. I attended a trip to Beijing, China, on behalf of the NBA and observed their preparation for the Beijing Olympics. They were building and reconstructing the city to prepare for the Olympic games. I saw the layout and brought the NBA relationship closer to the Chinese.

# "Antawn Jamison, Shaq, and I were selected as ambassadors."

The Chinese people were warm and welcoming, and the trip was a huge success. My wife, Nikkollette, went with me. We toured the Great Wall and Tiananmen Square, where Antawn and I conducted a basketball camp with about 300 young basketball players. We had a great time. I saw the beauty and importance of stepping into the role of an NBA Global Ambassador.

My brother and I would go on to serve alongside some of the league's most caring athletes in different regions of the world. I knew that every step I took would be like me aiming for change and shooting for peace. I learned so much from the opportunities to travel abroad with an amazing NBA staff. They would have everything planned out for us to make a meaningful difference. I may have retired from the court, but never from the role of serving a real purpose. So many moments have been memorable over the years, making up my retirement. I remember opening an envelope addressed to me from the White House. I was excited to open it as that's not a normal piece of mail I would pull from my mailbox. It was a letter from First Lady Laura Bush, thanking me for my service and the gifts I had left for her and President George Bush. My goal was to share three positive rap albums that Johnnie and I had co-produced with Steve Coleman, who was known as QTMC when he hit the stage. He had done a fantastic job of amplifying our encouraging messages in hip-hop songs that had kids rocking from the East to the West Coast. I often wonder if the president listened to our album.

As a parent who used to play pro ball before my daughters were somewhat aware of what was going on, I used to chuckle as they thought their dad knew everybody. On many occasions, we encountered old fans approaching for pictures and autographs. I am sure they have ever wondered what it must have been like during my moment. But I chose for them not to know, so that they could grow up with their own identities and have their dad at home much more than if I were still playing. Somehow, I knew I had made the right choice to walk away. The day my daughter Gabrielle walked across the graduation stage at Georgetown University, I heard her name called, and it felt like a championship win. As I write this memoir, my youngest daughter, Giselle, is celebrating her final year at Georgetown. She became an accomplished volleyball player. Hearing her name called out will be like adding another championship plaque in the air, and as parents, my wife and I will work to guide our son Jeremiah toward reaching his dreams.

*"All our kids are setting themselves up to play an amazing role."*

Jerome "JYD" Williams

# The White House

November 8, 2005

Dear Jerome,

*Thank you for coming to the White House Conference on Helping America's Youth and for supporting this important initiative. President Bush and I are grateful for your efforts to promote mentoring and to give children a positive outlook on their future.*

*Thank you also for the "Change the World and Mission Possible" CDs from your Quest to Make a Change program. I applaud you for spreading a positive, anti-violent message through music.*

*The President joins me in sending appreciation and best wishes.*

Sincerely,

## Laura Bush
The First Lady

## My Mission:

During this chapter of my life, I focused on preparing my family members to pursue their interests and continuing to find ways to challenge myself to be a positive example within my home and community.

## My Methods:

I chose to keep showing up each day. I wanted to ensure that each day, I would awaken to a purpose for the day and my time. Since leaving the court, I have kept an office within our home and one outside of my home. This was my main method for displaying my work ethic to our children. I stayed busy.

## My Measurables:

Ultimately, my greatest accomplishment has been pouring into my children, just as my parents took intentional time to do for me. As a result, they have each excelled. The private school expenses were covered, and now college degrees are going up on the wall.

# My 11ᵗʰ Role: Shooting For Peace

*"Sitting back watching the news and all the discourse between the community and police, I knew the retired NBA Legends could help bring some peace."*

I remember conversing with my brothers Johnnie and Joshua, where we recalled the impact I had made in cities I was fortunate to play in. We were on the road in Houston, Texas, and our table topic shifted from sports to what role athletes should play within their NBA cities. We explored some concepts that would've made an amazing viral video. I had just been assigned the role of president over the Young3.

This was the community outreach division for hip-hop artist Ice Cube. He had started a professional league for pro ballers to compete in half-court games, and we were tasked with managing his youth outreach. It was great to work with an amazing cast of retired ballers from the NBA, WNBA, Harlem Globetrotters, and Harlem Wizards.

They would help me execute a 3on3 experience the day before the official games. It was an amazing opportunity, but it also revealed much more work that needed to be done. My bigger vision was to connect with more athletes like myself, who now make up the retired NBA players' union. We have more time and some amazing stories about the different roads leading to our dreams. My years of experience serving the community gave me the vision to see all this endeavor could become.

My service to the community started at the Brewster-Wheeler Community Center in Detroit. This was my first camp for youth with my brother Johnnie. We offered an after-school program that pushed *books over balls* and a weekly skills clinic. Imagine over thirty young people sitting at tables doing their homework to be rewarded with practice sessions with me. Johnnie would run our practice like a pro session if I couldn't attend due to my travel schedule. These moments anchored me to my deep commitment to serve during the seasons I played and beyond.

Serving the youth brought me peace, which helped me wrestle with the frustration of not playing in the games. I wasn't playing in games, only in practice. So, in my world, I struggled to sustain inner peace. Basketball was always that place of peace, even if the games got chaotic.

I needed a distraction that would bring me some gratification and fulfillment. Helping others removed the focus from myself and placed my intention on being there for little people trying to win in life. It would bring me peace to see the frowns convert to smiles. In return for my small gestures of support, they each helped me see how blessed I was, which was a gift beyond measure.

My brother arranging this opportunity for me to support some younger athletes who he knew would be inspired to participate merely because I was a Detroit Piston was the beginning of it all. He would say, "They might stop you from making fans, but they can't stop me from making you some friends."

Statements like that would have me shaking my head, thinking that Johnnie was a dreamer with big ideas that were well-meaning but, at the moment, just seemed like words. He was an activist who had come to this life to serve, teach, and inspire, and I was about to benefit from having him on my team. I would get home from practice, tired and frustrated, and he would be there waiting to blitz me with information about students dropping out of school at alarming rates.

# "Shooting for Peace was birthed from that initial game."

We started to engage with more community partners. I began to get many community awards, which led to my receiving the NBA Community Service Award, presented by Fannie Mae. All the buzz about my work in the community led to me being featured on NBA Inside Stuff. Word was that Jerome Williams had a financial literacy program, which they featured on national television. And then I was featured again on NBA Inside Stuff for all of volunteerism. I was being featured for giving up the time I had available. The NBA and people throughout the community looked at my effort as something unique that deserved to be honored and promoted. But I was doing what my parents had always done and had expected from me.

During the summer of my first season, the NBA extended an opportunity to its players that would allow them to participate in a summer internship at the league office. From my perspective, the purpose of doing this was to allow players to learn about all the NBA departments that make the engine work. So, being the opportunist I was, my sports lawyer signed me up, and when I arrived, it was just me. I intended to meet all the staff at the NBA office. This experience offered me a deeper understanding of the infrastructure of how the league office worked, how they marketed players, and how they generated the player features for TV. The NBA staff member assigned to oversee my experience was Adam Silver (current NBA commissioner).

I was there to see the plans for activating David Sterns's vision for NBA Cares and let them know of my interest in helping drive it forward. The league began with activating its "Read to Achieve" initiative, which primarily focused on combating youth dropping out of school and youth illiteracy. They wanted to promote the benefits of reading to young NBA fans.

So, I figured I would offer my support and allow the league to leverage the fact that I had gotten a solid education and earned my degree before being drafted. I also had my brother, who had been looking at ways to engage students around the topic of reading, and he had already begun my motivational assembly tour. Imagine a team of musicians and dancers exciting students about school in between motivational remarks by my brother. Before leaving, every student and staff member would receive an autographed picture of me and my JYD mascot. We were ready!

Throughout my NBA journey, I solicited help from amazing people working in the community. One guy that comes to mind is Steve Coleman, also known worldwide as QTMC. He was a major part of the Detroit Pistons palace patrol, which engaged the fans. Johnnie discovered he was a rapper who performed educational and inspirational shows at schools and conferences. So, we sought his help writing lyrics to a Read to Achieve hip-hop anthem. We had no idea where it would take us, but we knew the kids would love it.

That initial project became the first of three albums we would have him produce for us. There was 'Read to Achieve,' 'Mission Possible,' and 'Change the World.' Our positive music was circulated in each NBA city that I played, from Detroit to Toronto, to Chicago, to New York. Johnnie and Steve hosted over 200 JYD assemblies in schools.

QTMC and I even performed our 'Read To Achieve' song at the Houston NBA All-Star Jam Fest. Word of my work made it to the president's desk at the time, and I was invited to the White House two times. My first trip was for a steak dinner, and I was seated at the table the president chose to eat at. My second visit was in association with a Bush Administration academic initiative. They recruited me for a project focused on education, but I respectfully declined due to scheduling conflicts.

The NBA gave me the opportunity to meet former President George Bush. I feel they chose me based on my community work off the court. I got to dine at the White House with my wife, Nikkollette. I wasn't political, but Johnnie always told me my role was to take our passion for serving youth to places he and other community organizers could not access. Those dinners were a tremendous honor because the typical pathway to the White House would require that I win an NCAA or NBA championship. For me, this was a different kind of championship. My work around the country had reached a level that Johnnie had always spoken of.

# "Throughout my career, I got multiple NBA CARES awards of the month."

Our phone line was literally ringing all the time once we began promoting my JYD Project. It was both the name of my nonprofit organization and the theme for our five-year social initiative. I looked at how many fans we were reaching each season and determined that with my growing popularity, NBA salary, and corporate partners, we could reach a half million youth over five years. My brand had been built around me simply doing what came naturally. I also had my brother heading up my public relations and social outreach. Because this took place before the explosion of the internet, Johnnie and QTMC were busy every day while I was at practice or playing games. But, I could make such a lofty claim with them engaging more than five thousand youth each week.

Although my NBA career ended before we completed our mission, I leveraged the extra time to join them to complete the work, and we did... I was even able to merge my passion for service with my love for cars. I participated in an annual celebrity car rally back in Toronto, which was very successful. It was a fun way to raise money. So, I activated my own JYD Celebrity Car Rally in Las Vegas and invited other retired NBA players to join me.

The invitations would lead to forming a Vegas chapter of the National Basketball Retired Players Association. We went on to become one of the most active members. I also shared with my peers how to build their brands while doing kind things. We began visiting hospitals, volunteering at homeless shelters, speaking at schools, and distributing food during November. We were displaying the NBA Cares, maybe even more in retirement, because we had more time.

But it wasn't until numerous police shootings became public that I would see value in us promoting "shooting for peace." Tragedy after tragedy began generating viral attention. When Freddie Gray sustained fatal injuries after his arrest, and then other males of color were shot and killed, I felt we had to do something. And then, I got a call to participate in a celebrity basketball game in Baltimore, Maryland. They were concerned about police getting gunned down in retaliation for what had happened. The news was stirring the frenzy with daily updates and troublesome images. So, I was asked to join some retired NFL and NBA players in lending our influence to help calm specific neighborhoods. The hope was that the young folks might still look up to us and local organizations could position our influence to promote peace.

When I arrived, they gave me a T-shirt titled "Shooting 4 Peace. And I was like, wow, that's a pretty cool slogan. But I didn't think too much of it beyond that. As I started talking to the community advocates, they provided information about what was happening in the neighborhood. I heard some painful stories about what had been going on for years and why they were fed up. Now, they were ready to shoot back. I knew that was not going to bring peace. I started thinking of what could be done. This was our opportunity to hear these young people and connect with these young adults. We had to bring the two sides together to discuss peace. But, from my years working with Johnnie, I had come to learn that trauma is trapped energy that we must be delicate when dealing with, so I decided we play together before talking to one another.

I felt there was something there, and we had to do better at leveraging the game of basketball to activate the concept of "Shooting for Peace." I knew I would need to fund it under my JYD Project, but I needed to discuss this with the NFL player who had hosted the game. I played in the celebrity game, and it helped calm the neighborhood. So, I decided to partner with my longtime friend, Charles "Choo" Smith, who had been the global ambassador of the Harlem Globetrotters. His impact within the city of Baltimore was stellar, and he crafted the vision and mission. When that was accomplished, we invited the original organizers to continue scheduling more games, but their schedules couldn't accommodate hosting games in different markets. But they weren't as interested in getting into the work of trying to create programs and a scalable initiative. So, I said to myself. If anybody can do this, it's me. I know too much. I have too much experience. And. If not me, then who?

# *"This was my moment to step up big."*

I started to develop my own programs, whereas, in the past, Johnnie had developed them for me. He was now busy with speaking contracts, and it was up to me to continue my legacy within the community. My mother would come to assist me for a time, and my dad was the star of all of my sports camps. But I missed having that partner in service and was fortunate to welcome Bryan Burrell to my team to help me grow in this next chapter. Together, we would seek new partners. He would oversee my projects and the creation of a basketball media company that has captured hundreds of hours of great content. We looked at education partners like Everfi, which had a digital education platform with partnerships already in place. Working with them allowed me to fund thousands of high schoolers to access the country by accessing financial literacy content and black history information.

This organizational growth led to a conversation with my wife about creating scholarship opportunities for students to access year after year. So, we established a student scholarship at Montgomery College, where my journey began, but we quickly realized that so many students needed help paying the rising costs of college. I couldn't do this alone, but I was relentless in seeking a way to scale my support for young people pursuing higher education. I had heard that many Historically Black Colleges and Universities (HBCUs) had scholarships and grant money going unutilized. So, I called on a colleague who had connections with HBCUs. They connected me with a guy named Dr. Smith down at Alabama State University. He allocated some of his scholarship funds to be offered to youth participating in Shooting for Peace.

We awarded over a half million dollars in scholarships in New Orleans the first year. That was a huge milestone because it began to wake up other players. They started to see that we still had power that we could leverage for youth. And by locking arms with me, we could change the world. Bryan and I started to get more chapters involved and leaned into the Shooting for Peace program. We have activated the initiative in Detroit, Atlanta, Houston, New York, LA, Las Vegas, Chicago, and other cities nationwide. Year after year, we gave out hundreds of thousands of dollars in scholarships to kids through our Shooting or Peace program.

As a role player, I have learned this was my most important assignment. The opportunities that I have leveraged have been made possible by my NBA opportunity. Without it, I wouldn't have been able to reach back to the community and help so many. I wouldn't be able to tell youth, "I made it, and you can do it, too." I came into this world and took the gifts the Lord gave me to serve as best I could. I accepted my role. It wasn't as glamorous as Michael Jordan's, Dr. J's, Allen Iverson's, or Kobe Bryant's. But I wouldn't change a thing if I could.

As I move forward, I haven't stopped meeting presidents. I spoke with President Obama while he was in office and was recently invited to the White House with my son to participate in an NBA fit event under President Joe Biden. Jeremiah and I played a little basketball with other youth. It was an incredible feeling to shoot some baskets with my son on the south lawn of the White House. It made me think of how far my father's principles and hard work had gotten me. Just watching him taking shots like it was just another day reminded me of how far each role had taken me.

My hope is that you catch the ball of opportunity and engage with others peacefully as we all aim for the dreams we chase. We have raised over $10 million in scholarships, and each year, we find a way to give even more. Now, I visit my brother, Johnnie, in Chicago, where I used to play. He has found yet another way for us to do something unique for the community, leveraging our wisdom. Now, we have both lived over a half-century and are planning to anchor our legacies in such a way that our systems aid the community in uplifting itself.

## My Mission:

During this chapter of my life, my role was to create new programs and initiatives that could make a difference. I also focused on selecting new teammates to aid me in scaling my service efforts.

## My Methods:

In my opinion, the most impactful method for making a difference begins with showing up to do what is needed when it is required. So, if I placed something on my schedule, I worked hard to fulfill all my promises to continue to build and sustain community trust.

## My Measurables:

Aside from living a very fulfilling life, I have begun to cross paths with fans from my past who now have kids and families of their own. It is humbling to see folks show me they still have pictures I signed when they were young, over twenty years ago. The good vibes never get old.

# My 12<sup>th</sup> Role: Passing The Wisdom

*"The Junk Yard Dog is known as just Rome. He is my big brother, who took the time to teach me some much-needed life lessons that saved my NBA career as a player."*

-Allen Iverson HOF

As I have gotten older, I have learned that the most valuable asset is the wisdom someone will pass along to you. I say that because it takes time to gain knowledge. You can save time and maybe resources by leveraging someone else's experience. I had to learn over the years that the wisdom I took time to learn from the veterans saved me from making so many mistakes that could have cost me everything. And, the sad reality came as I watched peers too stubborn to ask or listen begin to fail or struggle through mistakes the older guys had tried to warn us about. Take a moment to think about what I just said.

I want to share an example of how Johnnie and I have begun leveraging technology to connect with students who wish to ask me questions. We scheduled a Zoom call with a group of young men from Chicago who are each members of the CHAMPS Male Mentoring program.

# Zoom@Noon
# w/guest Jerome Williams:

## Johnnie Williams III: (meeting host)

Good day, champs! Today, one of my younger brothers is with us. Jerome, whom you all can call JYD, is joining us to answer any questions you might wish to ask about striving for your dreams.

So, gentlemen, make sure you think about the questions you will ask. Then, listen to how he answers your question and what you will do with the wisdom he passes to you. Ask questions that will take you forward. For any questions, you can just Google; consider not asking that. Take full advantage of this *Ask the Pro* session. It is okay if somebody asks the same thing you were going to say. Do not be discouraged; ask something else.

Okay, somebody jump in and introduce yourself.

> *"I enjoy passing the wisdom great coaches poured into me. Now coaching and public speaking offer me that game time feeling I have been looking for."*

## Jaylin:

What was your motivation? My challenge is that I need some motivation in life.

## Jerome JYD Williams:

I like that question, Jaylin. Motivation comes from within, and to your point, you won't feel up to it every day. You might not have the same energy daily, but it is more about mindset.

That was one thing I learned to strengthen when I was your age. I was taught to train my mind at home and in various sports. I had to get up and do things I was not motivated at times to do. But school was where I had to apply inner drive and motivation the most. We go to school to learn, right? We go to school to achieve, get the grades, and reach our goals. But we're also there to strengthen our minds. You must practice holding positive thoughts – so you can hold positive thoughts during challenging or inconvenient moments. The way to overcome moments when you lack motivation is to figure out what you want so badly that everything you must endure to access it is worth it. That is what will drive you when your inner fuel is low.

And sometimes, the distance to your desired destination seems so far away that you judge yourself for being where you are. Don't do that to yourself; instead, say these words: "Where I am is not who I am. It's just where I am. Because who I am is greater than where I am." Jaylin, I want you to repeat that to yourself when you feel uninspired to continue. Then, think of what you want for yourself and proceed despite feeling low. Go onto YouTube, type in motivation, and listen to the positive messages that offer hope when needed. Eventually, the inspiration will need to come from within.

## Myron:

I think I will ask you about making the right college decision. How did you know you picked the right college or university?

## Jerome JYD Williams:

That was one of the toughest decisions because it was monumental. Some people have lots of options to choose from, and others have very few. Sometimes, other factors like distance and fees make the choice easier or harder. But for me, the dilemma you speak of came after graduating from a local junior college. I had gotten my associate's degree and now had to choose between two schools offering me a scholarship.

I feel like everything in life eventually comes down to two options, and selecting to go either way comes with its pros and cons. So, let me share what happened when I dealt with what you just asked. I had a basketball scholarship in my hand. It was to attend American University. That was an outstanding school, and it had an okay basketball program. Has anybody here on this call ever heard of American University in basketball?

No! So, they were pretty much unknown. And I was truly excited to attend when they were my only option for remaining close to home. But then, I was presented with the same opportunity from Georgetown University. Now, they had a major basketball program that had produced NBA players. Now, I'm sitting there trying to decide which side of the fence was right for me.

The choice was mine to make. At American Univ., I'd be the team captain and run the show. But the thing is, it would be a smaller show. On the other hand, Georgetown already had a talented roster of players, and I might be lucky to get on the court at all. The coursework was some of the most rigorous in the country. So, I had to make that decision. Myron, brother, I was sweating bullets. I had people like my brother in my ear saying, Look, man. What are you going to do? I'm like, man. I don't know if I can handle the pressure at Georgetown. But by going there, I get the chance to reach my dream. It was also going to be the most challenging path for me to take.

I had to look away from option A and option B. I thought about the fact that either school would help me get a great job. However, only one of them would bring me closer to what I really wanted, and that was how the decision was made. I left my comfort zone at that table and didn't think I ever returned to retrieve it. As a result of my choice, I realized my dream, but it was not simple. I didn't choose the easy path. So, I say trust yourself and look deeply at which option seems to present the greatest challenge and which will deliver your reward as a result of passing all the tests. Myron, when I made that decision,

I faced some tough hurdles but kept climbing. I stayed motivated and dedicated. And I kept my mindset right to reach my ultimate goal.

## Mikel:

What would have been your plan B if you had not made it to the NBA?

## Jerome JYD Williams:

You're talking my language, Mikel. You see, at Georgetown, we had some of the best internships in Washington, DC. Area. So, in the summer of my junior year, I secured an internship paying me $10 an hour (back in 1996). I played the role of a tax clerk for Arthur Anderson, one of the country's largest accounting firms. They managed billions of dollars back in the 90's, and my job was to handle any fax that came in and deliver it to the proper accounting department. And then, by the end of the day, after all the deposits had been collected, I had to deliver checks from clients to the IRS.

Now, these checks had to be there by 4 PM daily. So, it was my job to collect every check that needed to be taken and hand-deliver them. Now I had my choice in how to get there, as long as I was on time.

I could catch a cab or walk, but it was about a mile from our office. Well, one thing I found out on my 1st day attempting to catch a cab in Washington, DC, it was rather tricky to get a cab to stop and pick me up. I guess I appeared too tall to fit their ideal customer profile. So, there was an obstacle I had to figure out for myself, but I had a job to get done. So, I walked every day. I just planned to make sure I had 15 to 20 minutes to hustle down there. Granted, I was in a suit, so I had to take care not to sweat too much.

But I was always on time and always made it by that 4 PM deadline. At the end of the internship, the firm offered me a full-time job after graduation from Georgetown. Their job offer started at over $50,000 a year right out of college, which was good money at the time. So, with plan B secured, I went all in on my plan A, and the cool thing is...I had a choice between the two options.

Great question, Mikel.

## Corde:

I want to ask what you want to be remembered for?

## Jerome JYD Williams:

That was good...What do I want to be remembered for?

Well, let me dive in. I am writing a book to help me pass the wisdom I have received. I was a role player in the NBA. I was asked to hold back some of my talents and step into less glamorous roles. But I leveraged my positive mindset. And I want to share what I know in a way that can help some of you. I do not think I am too concerned with being remembered as much as I want you to remember so many of the things I hope to pass along so that you reach your dream. But I think most folks will remember my positive attitude.

I want to share something that happened during my rookie year. I was very upset. You could say I was in a funk. I was unhappy. I was mad because I wasn't playing. In my mind, I was supposed to be playing the game I loved. I was getting paid to prepare and then sit on the bench. I had reached my dream of being drafted, but because of the deep roster and nature of the business, I didn't get to play. Sometimes, I had to say I was hurt when I wasn't. That upset me even more. Meanwhile, in practice, I was running laps around the guys. I was full of energy. I could get to the balls faster. I was more athletic. I could jump over the top of many of them. I could score at will, but they wouldn't let me on the court, which frustrated me. So, one day, I said, you know what? I am not smiling anymore.

I got called into the general manager's office. He asked that I sit down, and then he asked. Jerome, what's the problem today? You have not been your usual energetic self. You're not as positive. You're not out there high-fiving everybody. You're not, you know, out here giving it your same level of energy. And I said, well, you know why? Because I'm not playing. I don't feel like smiling. I do not feel I offer any value here. So basically, I'm unmotivated to be in a good mood. But I am here doing my job. I said I'm tired of doing it with a smile and trying to lift everybody else up.

"Wait, stop right there." He said, "We drafted you and signed you to a contract, not just because of your rebounding, scoring, or passing. We signed you because of your level of positive energy and how it'd help uplift our organization. So, if you're not willing to continue that same effort, then let us know so we can make other arrangements for you." I was like, *"Whoa! Wait a minute. What? What are we talking about here? Like a trade?"*

So, I quickly said to myself and then to him. *"Oh, no, it's not a problem."* I had to recalibrate my mindset and, to Jaylin's point, find my motivation. I want to be remembered as someone willing to give the extra. I want to be remembered as one of the great role players. The guy willing to be a relentless opportunist who leveraged everything around me to help myself and others. I'm playing my role on this call. I'm answering your questions. I'm being present, and I'm listening to each and every one of you. So, you see the value in yourselves that your mentors do.

## John:

Seeing the age range of everybody on this call being 15-18.

What is one thing, or one word, that you have said to inspire yourself to prepare for the future?

## Jerome JYD Williams:

I love that question, John, and my one word is simply DISCIPLINE. My dad and mom stressed it daily at the age you all are now. *"Jerome, you have to be more disciplined."*

Discipline is that routine that you stick with and never break from— making up my bed every day, doing my chores, taking out the garbage, and washing the dishes. It was applying effort to the little things I didn't want to do/that taught it. How many of you guys have your own bedroom? First, I had to share my bedroom with my brother. Then I got my own room. Well, it required discipline to take care of it without being told. You see, a young man with self-discipline requires very little input from adults, feeling they need to discipline him.

My day still begins with a simple discipline that started way back when I was younger. When I wake up each day, I make the bed before leaving my home. It is so much of a habit that I even make it up at the hotels I stay in. They say that people making their bed daily are some of the most highly successful people on the planet. But discipline is one of my three favorite words beginning with "D." Dedication is first, determination is second, and discipline concludes the three. John, be disciplined, brother.

## Nasir:

My question is, what are some key lessons you've learned from (actual) life?

## Jerome JYD Williams:

Nasir, the key life lesson I learned was to keep the faith. At times, it can be challenging to find your faith, and other circumstances might cause you to lose it.

Life taught me that faith in a higher power would offer stability throughout my life, which I have found to be accurate. Throughout my career, I attended chapel service before just about every game in every NBA city I played. I made a lot of money in my career, and every dollar in my pocket has said, "IN GOD WE TRUST." And I never wanted to forget that my Christian faith challenged me to keep some very important commandments that have added to the good in my life. I have never forgotten all the prayers I sent out for more height, to pass a test, to win a game, or to have a safe flight to Chicago this morning to speak with you all. I never allowed the money to disconnect me from my source and savior Jesus Christ

Life has also taught me the importance of finding faith in myself. It can become very easy to have faith in the unseen or even others we rely upon. But I think the game of basketball demanded that with each shot I took, I have faith in myself and my ability to hit the shot. And, even if I missed it, I needed to sustain faith in my ability to make the next one. I think that inner faith is a flame you must light and keep burning throughout your life. I'm not sure what you all want from life, but I am sure that there will come moments that feel bigger than you. At these moments, I want you to trust that you are divinely covered and that everything will work out. But there will also come some moments that you must grow emotionally, intellectually, and spiritually. Don't avoid the work you must do; trust your vision and chase your dreams. That's a good question, Nasir.

## Mahfuz:

My question is, what type of mindset did you develop to reach your goals?

## Jerome JYD Williams:

That is another great question that requires me to think about what state of mind helped me achieve most of my goals.

My mindset wasn't as consistent as I would have wanted it to be. Based on the circumstances and how I felt on any given day, I would say that setting my mind on autopilot was the key. I say that because I feel that my mindset was connected to what I intended to do. But some days, I did not want to do what was so important just a few days earlier. So, this is what I want you to do to achieve your goals.

First, I want you to make your goal clear and concise so you know your destination. Second, I need for you to create a plan or play to achieve the goal. The bigger the goal, the more detailed the plans for reaching it. Third, I want you to practice the actual steps or routine to bring your goal towards completion. Your "process" needs to become a habit that will aid you in achieving much more than just a mindset alone. For example, Kobe Bryant had the Mamba Mentality, which most believe was his winning mindset. But take it from someone who got drafted with him. I played against him and had to guard him. His daily habits produced his performance outcomes. Those habits supported his winning mindset.

So, I want to pass you the wisdom of going even deeper than the surface. Root your efforts deep enough for your dreams to grow. Great question, Mahfuz.

## Jeremy:

How did you deal with the tough times before the NBA draft and the money that came to you? Did you believe the struggle was temporary and that you could still see the light?

## Jerome JYD Williams:

Jeremy, that's a powerful question…

Honestly, it never really appeared like I was going to make it until I heard my name called. There were so many obstacles that I just got used to trying my best, and that process kept opening new doors that kept offering me more hope. But that hope always seemed to draw another challenge. So, the light that was already in me, and I just began to find joy in the moment I was in or the game I was playing.

Life is always right now, and my dream came true in a moment of now. But many people played a role in helping me, and others played a role in trying to stop or discourage me. Their defense allowed me to practice getting around it. I became a pro at getting through challenges before I became a pro at playing basketball. That is why I'm writing 'ROLE Player,' so that questions like yours can be answered, one chapter at a time.

Just keep placing one foot in front of the other despite the resistance ahead. And embrace the discomfort of stretching yourself. Go to school with the intention of stretching your mind in each class. Dedicate yourself to learning each day, and I believe you'll be okay.

## Coach Derrick James:

My question would be, what would you say is your purpose?

## Jerome JYD Williams:

My purpose in life is to help people find their peace while they're here. We shouldn't continue to connect the concept of "rest in peace" to an afterlife. We should live in peace along the way.

So, throughout my career, I played an aggressive sport that required us to tip-toe the line of imposing our power without overpowering another. We clash with each other without intending to hurt one another. So, you can imagine how often tempers might fly. When this would happen, my role was to step in between as a neutral barrier to disrupt the explosion and help re-establish the calm that allowed the game to continue. I have taken this effort into communities and countries where peace has been lost or is on the brink.

I would have never assumed that that would be my purpose, but it is something that comes most naturally to me. For instance, I'm in Chicago today to support my man Joakim Noah's "One City League." It aims to promote peace and decrease the violence across the city. Then, I'm headed to a basketball court dedication with Operation Basketball, which is focused on the same. Then, I believe I'll check out Project Swish, which was started by a passionate young man who lost a close friend to gun violence.

That's why I have my brother Johnnie positioned in Chicago. He will be seeking partners for my Shooting for Peace initiative. I feel that promoting peace is my real purpose.

## Coach Derrick James:

Live in peace, right?

## Jerome JYD Williams:

Live in peace, brother...

## Johnnie Williams III:

CHAMPS, I am proud of the questions you have posed to my brother, and I hope you have taken his responses to heart. Go and play your role with relentless optimism, and leverage everything.

# My Mission:

I decided to stop what I was doing and dedicate an hour of my time to answering the questions of young people aspiring to reach their dreams. I look forward to continuing to host these pro chats each month for future stars shooting for a dream.

# My Methods:

I have learned to leverage technology platforms that link me to students in other cities and countries. I allow my life experiences to serve as examples of what can be accomplished with perseverance and self-belief. I focus on being as honest as I can and also share some of my stumbles and fumbles.

# My Measurables:

I believe we connected with youth some might feel are no longer listening or engaging. The questions these teenagers asked me really made me think deeply. I believe a difference was made, and hopefully, I said something that offered value to them and you, too.

# My 13ᵗʰ Role: Let's Talk NIL

*"Seeing my name highlighted in our national paper was the most amazing feeling. This sent a message to my kids about the importance of me reinventing myself."*

As I focused more and more on the values that comprise my story, it became apparent that I had to pass on the wisdom. I sat with my team and discussed what was best for me to share. Around this time, I connected with my good friend and Georgetown alumni Stephen Borrelli about my vision for assisting other athletes like myself to learn about and leverage their NIL opportunities. He felt that my IPFAMBA app platform was both newsworthy and noteworthy. Our conversation manifested into a great article that the folks at USA Today approved me sharing.

**Former NBA player Jerome Williams says young athletes should market themselves early:**

---

## Stephen Borelli

USA TODAY

As a basketball player, Jerome Williams was known as the Junkyard Dog, or "JYD," a nod to his ferocious nature in the paint and in cleaning up rebounds.

It's a marketable name that Williams now plays up on social media. He got his nickname in the NBA, but Williams had enough of a reputation as a sturdy 6-foot-9 power forward at Georgetown to have his own trading card in college.

"The revenue streams from that, I can't really see because the NCAA signed deals with those trading card companies to be able to monetize my image, name, and likeness without me getting a dime from that because I had signed my letter of intent with Georgetown," says Williams, who helped the Hoyas reach the Sweet 16 in 1995 and the Elite Eight in 1996.

Williams, who retired after a nine-year NBA career in 2005, thinks back to his playing days about how he could have marketed himself in today's college basketball world. It's a world that is now being shaped by an NCAA rules change that followed the passage of state laws permitting student athletes to capitalize on their name, image and likeness (NIL).

Among many ventures and initiatives, Williams has been an ambassador for the game overseas, a high school basketball coach in Las Vegas and an advocate for the NBA's retired players in promoting and protecting their legacies. At 50, he is now honing in on the sports-playing kids like he once was through his company, Intellectual Property For Athletes Made By Athletes or IP FAMBA.

Among a number of offerings, his company generates an IP score, which takes data on athletes, including where they live, what sport they play, their grade point average, their social media following and awards. There is also a social platform where they can post as part of a community with other athletes.

He isn't waiting until boys and girls are in college, though, to understand and promote their NIL.

"Sixth grade is when we tell kids to start getting going; some as early as fifth grade because a lot of the major sports really start scouting the sixth grade," he tells USA TODAY Sports. "So, basketball, football, you're already being rated and ranked in these grades, and that includes tennis and other sports from volleyball to cheerleading."

Williams hosted a Future Pros basketball event this weekend in Washington, D.C., open to middle school boys and girls of all talent levels. The session offered circuit training and instruction from former professionals, including Williams, but also an off-court class for parents and players about the NIL landscape.

Every artifact from one's sports career - such as memorabilia, photo, or videos - can be preserved as "intellectual property" in a digital portfolio. Williams' middle-school aged son, Jeremiah, for example, has collected keepsakes from basketball tournaments around the country as part of his digital scrapbook.

"I want other parents to understand what they could be doing with their kids, too," he says.

These items, he says, can one day help you monetarily (through bids from family, friends, and fans) but also boost your exposure and NIL profile as a player rising the sports pyramid, which gets narrower and narrower as you move from middle school to high school and college.

"Let's say you're on a football team in high school and you are one of the top-ranked teams in your county," Williams says, "and you win a lot of games and you start to create your data collection. Well, chances are you have fans in your neighborhood, in your community, that want to support you."

Williams has a holistic view of the young athlete. He is a father of four and a sports dad. Two of his daughters, Gabby and Giselle, are on the volleyball team at Georgetown. He has learned through parenting athletes and his own experience that the most important components of a kid who aspires to play in high school, college and beyond are time and commitment.

Williams' own parents didn't have the means for camps or personal instruction, as he has found for Gabby and Giselle. Instead, his dad spent endless hours with him on the basketball court. Such dedication overcompensated for any knowledge he lacked.

Here are five tips from him on how to use the valuable time we have as parents of youth athletes to promote their careers while enhancing their lives.

## 1. Discover their love for a sport

"I think the No. 1 focus is making sure that they are doing what they love to do," Williams says. "Also, not pushing them beyond their own limits of how much they want to put into this sport."

In middle school, Williams played soccer and ran cross country but then realized he wanted to zero in on basketball. He recommends you have your son or daughter specialize in a sport by the seventh or eighth grade if they are serious about playing it in college.

He did so with his kids in sixth grade.

"That's the time when they start to develop, they start to grow and you can have a better sense of some of their strengths if you're looking at one sport," he says. "When they were in fourth, fifth grade, they were playing tennis, volleyball and track and field so it was sort of like, 'Man they're decent at all of 'em but what are they gonna enjoy playing the most?' So, I let them choose and then we just focused on that one thing for sixth, seventh and eighth grade." In this space, I have written about how a kid committing too early to one sport can contributing to burnout. That burnout, Williams says, comes from overzealous parents.

"There's a fine line between someone who's trying to do something as a young person and someone who's being pushed to do something by a parent. ... You have to make sure that there's 100 percent buy-in all the time. And that can change from week to week but you have to allow that change to take place because you can't have a child or a young athlete feeling like this is your dream because that's when you can run into problems."

## 2. Do the work and remember: 'You can't create a kid like yourself'

Williams admits his knowledge of basketball has helped his son, but he didn't play volleyball and never trained his daughters at the sport.

"You can't create a kid like yourself," he says. "You can't make them to be like you or want the same things that you want."

If you can't afford to pay a private coach, you can find drills to mimic from coaches and professionals on the internet to help you learn a sport.

"It just boils down to how much time you want to spend with your kid," Williams says. "How did I make it? I was just out on the basketball court and my dad was throwing me the ball."

Williams' father didn't offer much instruction, other than "make sure you hold your follow-through." But before YouTube or Instagram, he was there with his son when he needed him, taking pride in learning the game himself through relentless repetition.

## 3. Know the odds

According to recent figures, close to 500,000 athletes compete in NCAA sports. If that sounds like a large number, consider there are about 8 million high school athletes.

Williams believes in putting those odds in perspective for kids.

"Let them know, 'Hey, in order to be a volleyball Division I athlete ... you're gonna have to do the work and you're gonna have to make yourself visible to the point where you stand out. That is learning the sport, taking time to be trained in the sport correctly. ... It's a little bit of a cheat code in terms of being able to give my son everything that I know (in basketball), but it's still up to him how far he wants to take it because, at that level, it's a lot tougher competition."

Or perhaps, when your son or daughter gets to high school or college, they realize they are doing a sport because it is something they enjoy. They might want to play that sport on an intramural or recreational level in college because it is still an enriching activity for them.

## 4. Promote your unique self

Most collegiate (and professional) athletes will tell you that unless you're physically gifted, like Williams' college roommate, Allen Iverson, all of those hours you put in at your sport are what will separate you from the crowd.

"Those hours that you split between two (sports), it's gonna be hard for you to compete against the kid that's spending all of his hours with just one," Williams says.

Grades are crucial, too. Coaches and schools are monitoring them. You can put yourself even more on these schools' radars if you distinguish yourself academically.

Another way to get coaches' attention is through social media posts about your achievements. (Personal tip: Don't brag too much. Before either of my sons, who are 16 and 13, makes a social media post, I proofread for misspellings and to make sure they are representing themselves respectfully and accurately.

Building up your list of followers can help you get NIL deals down the road, too, Williams says. Just don't let the activity consume you.

## 5. Set limits with devices

Video games, like social media and phone consumption, don't end. They are a continuum of distraction unless you nip them in the bud.

It's hard to compete for a spot on a high school or college team with a kid who puts in four hours a day five times a week at their craft when your kid puts in one hour. If your kids are serious about his or her athletic craft, don't let them get sucked into technology that keeps them from it.

"Sometimes you gotta take the phone away," Williams says. "Monitor your kids' internet, monitor your kids' video games. My advice is monitor, and keep monitoring and keep setting limits."

Don't give in when they push back.

"Oh, just five more minutes, Dad," Jeremiah told him the other day. "If I quit the game now, I lose all of my tokens."

"What does that have to do with you getting off the phone?" Williams said. "They lock these kids into something that keeps them on these games that ultimately takes time away from doing something productive."

During a family vacation, Williams noticed his son constantly looking at his phone. It was a good reminder to all of us that sometimes we get distracted about what is important, in sports and in life.

"I had to take away his phone just so he could walk around and see his surroundings and see what's out there," Williams says. "You're not gonna see anything with these phones ... The phone is gonna be there, the game is gonna be there, social media is gonna be there.

"I think when parents first viewed it, it was something that gave them some time so that they could do things they wanted to do because your kid was occupied by this phone.

"You're trying to get some of that time back."

> *This article was originally published at USATODAY.com on Aug. 20, 2023.*
>
> *Steve Borelli, aka Coach Steve, has been an editor and writer with USA TODAY since 1999. He spent 10 years coaching his two son's baseball and basketball teams. He and his wife, Colleen, are now loving life as sports parents for two high schoolers.*

---

I have got to be honest. It felt amazing to be interviewed about my vision for helping to empower other athletes by capturing the equity within their personal brands and for Steve to put together such an extensive piece for USA TODAY in August 2023.

Just think of how often a retired NBA player, 19 years removed from the game, justifies this type of press coverage. So, I must thank the team at USA TODAY that reviewed my request to release their entire (published) article to be included in my book 'ROLE Player.' I didn't know what to expect, and neither did Steve, but the worst the answer could have been was "no."

## *[R] relentless [O] opportunists [L] leverage [E] everything*

Allow this article to serve as more validation for you to consider; if you don't ask for it, it will most likely not be given. I want you to know that I ask myself each day what role I can play and how I can conclude this day as a better version of myself than the version of Jerome from the day before.

I sincerely hope you have caught the passes I dished your way...

"Jerome was the Kevin Durant in DC before KD"
- Allen Iverson, HOF

# The Legends Speak

*"I consider it a true blessing to reach for my phone and call up some of the greatest players to ever play and hear some of the things they had to say about me."*

My parents would often say to me, "Jerome, you never know who is watching you." And they couldn't have been more correct. I had teachers, friends, coaches, NBA scouts, and the public watching me. So, their timeless suggestion was to practice being respectful and responsible. In doing this, I wouldn't burn any bridges or destroy relationships I may need to have later in life. Well, later has come, and I have been humbled by many of the comments some of my mentors and peers have had to say about me and my career. Know that people will also have great things to say about you, just as long as you played a solid role on their team or in their lives.

## Allen Iverson said...

The Junk Yard Dog is known to me as just ROME. He is my big bro who took the time to teach me some much-needed life lessons that saved my NBA career as a player. Jerome Williams deserves to be in the Basketball Hall of Fame as a Contributor because of the many players in the game he has stopped to help with his unique actions on and off the court. Basketball-wise, JYD was Kevin Durant before KD!

Humanitarian-wise, he was sent to me by God, and I'm forever grateful.

Allen "The Answer" Iverson – HOF

## Dr. J said...

"I knew there was something special when I met Jerome Williams at the age of 19 on a beach in Daytona, FL, where we battled 1-on-1. Throughout my many years as a basketball Hall of Famer, I've seen many great NBA players contribute, but JYD is one of the best Global Sports Ambassadors the game has had. He should be recognized for his contributions to the game as a global community activist shooting for peace. From the infectious energy that he brings to his tenacious attitude to help and encourage others around him, JYD deserves a major salute from his NBA brothers!"

Julius "Dr. J" Erving - HOF

## George Gervin said...

The Basketball Hall of Fame is missing a major contributor to the game named Jerome JYD Williams! Mr. Williams, aka the Junk Yard Dog, is the type of humanitarian the global game of basketball is proud of. I've worked with this heartfelt man on numerous occasions over the past 20 years. I watched him develop as a local Detroit Piston community contributor to his NBA global community outreach, real players and real people recognize. JYD is a real humanitarian and deserves to be honored in the HOF as a Contributor to the Game!

George "Iceman" Gervin – HOF

## Lenny Wilkins said...

What I valued about you was that I could count on you to make a difference and be ready to play when we needed you. When I put you in the game, I knew you would play your role and be prepared to help us. Any coach that wants to win must have people who understand their roles and how they fit in. You did that very well.

Lenny Wilkins – HOF

## Rick Barry said...

I love Jerome. He's truly a great guy with a great personality. He does many things to help kids out – it's inspiring. If you know Jerome, you'll know what a terrific guy he is and know that he's on the right track to the HOF.

Rick Barry – HOF

## Nancy Lieberman said...

I've known Jerome Williams for many years, and I'm always amazed by what he's done off the court to change the lives of children around the world. If more people would use their God-given abilities as assets to help others, then our world would be destined for greatness.

Nancy "Lady Magic" Lieberman, HOF, Class of '96

## Rick Mahorn said...

"You were one of the best at accepting situations, and the advice that I gave, you took it and made it your own. You still owe me some royalties on your JYD brand, which I was a part of birthing into existence. The respect I have for you is how you analyzed the value and potential of a playful nickname, and you turned it into your own identity and economy. In our league, you had to have an identity, and you built it up to take care of your family. All the little things you did have grown into big things."

Rick "The Bad Boy" Mahorn

## Charles Oakley said...

"JYD, the Junkyard Dog, would come in ready to put in the hard work. He was a guy that knew how to play and get his mind right for every game. And, I feel when the comparisons of guys like Dennis Rodman, myself, and Draymond Green come up, we were the role players that did the dirty work and gave our teams second chances and extra baskets. I include Jerome in that special group of players that just got the job done. I take my hat off to him. When he came to Toronto, he lived up to his hype, and he got the crowd going. Canadian fans love him, and I was honored to be one of the players he modeled his game after. And, we have been fortunate to work together in our post-NBA careers as well."

Charles "Oak" Oakley

## Don Sperling said...

If you have ever met and talked with Jerome Williams, your life has become a little brighter. "Junkyard Dog," as we know him, is a truly unique individual. We met at NBA Entertainment years back when he was one of our player correspondents for NBA Inside Stuff. To say Renaissance Man would only begin to scratch the surface. Yes, he had great basketball skills coming out of Georgetown University. However, he has risen above the game, putting his stamp on the world and everyone he meets. Jerome is a Global Ambassador for the game, and his charity and service is unparalleled. If you ever get the chance, I highly recommend exchanging some words with Jerome. It's like being touched by an angel.

Don Sperling D.S. – HOF (NBA, Inside Stuff)

# Growling In Gratitude

*"We have been steered to admire what offers us so very little in return and told to ignore the people and things that offer us so much real value."*

- Johnnie Williams III

I felt like I needed to conclude my memoir by expressing deep appreciation to twenty-six of the most valuable players in my life that have each played a role in shaping my career. I can honestly say that "Thank You" was the greatest tool I leveraged while reaching my dream. I kept thanking people, and they kept doing more and more for me. These next few pages are reserved for my appreciation to all the coaches and cheerleaders in my life:

**#1** I thank my parents, Johnnie & Seaquett who taught me how to be a responsible parent. Your examples of selflessness made the daily tasks seem simple, yet I better understood what you offered to me as I made the effort to offer my children the same.

**#2** I want to thank my wife, Nikkollette Williams, who captured my heart and never let it go. You have been that voice of reason, telling me things I didn't want to hear but you knew I needed to consider. You crowned me a champion when you placed that ring on my finger, and I knew I had won.

**#3** I want to thank my late grandmother, Fannie Emmert, who modeled for me the importance of attending church and practicing the expression of my faith.

**#4** I want to thank my elementary school teacher, Mrs. Kay from Montrose Christian School, for encouraging me to accept Jesus Christ.

**#5** I want to thank my grandfathers, Edward Ballard, Henry Emmert, and Johnnie Williams Sr., for showing me how dedication, determination, and discipline can pay off in big ways.

**#6** I want to thank my third-grade English teacher, Mrs Steutes. She would not let me settle for the status quo, and you helped to shift my perspective on getting an education.

**#7** I want to thank my amazing eighth-grade teacher, Mrs Piwko, from the Woods Academy. She motivated me to get through her class and made sure that I did the work. Her role in setting an expectation of effort and self-belief contributed greatly to my confidence in excelling in high school and college.

**#8** I want to thank coach Dan Harwood for dishing out the tough love that aided my perspective around practice and always being on time. You also taught me an invaluable life lesson about avoiding trouble and not associating with troublemakers. If you hadn't benched me for being present at a student fight, I may have learned the lesson later at the expense of reaching my dream.

**#9** I want to thank my great friend Kevin Herod for helping take my game to the next level. You shared the wisdom your father was passing you, which helped my game tremendously. You were my sharp shooter that allowed me to stay on the courts for hours and hours, getting the invaluable practice I needed. This was how I could compensate for all the basketball camps I did not attend. I am so happy to see you coaching collegiate athletes and helping them reach their personal goals.

**#10** I want to thank Coach Steve Hobson, my coach at Montgomery College. You pushed me to improve and withheld your praise until I truly earned it. I literally grew into a major college player right before your eyes. I will never forget the green light you offered me to average 27 points and 20 rebounds.

**#11** I want to thank Coach D (Darnell Myers), who served as my first talent scout, extracted me from the suburbs of Maryland and took me to the invitation-only gym that helped me earn my Georgetown University scholarship.

**#12** I want to thank Dr. Joe Carr for serving as my basketball mentor. You created a system to support emerging ball players and current college and professional players. Your selflessness and service to others inspired me to serve youth throughout my career in honor of the doors you opened for me.

**#13** I want to thank Coach John Thompson and all of the coaching staff at Georgetown University. I will forever appreciate the long hours you all put in to help prepare me for an NBA career. You took a chance on me and became the pathway and portal to my NBA dream. I cannot see myself getting drafted without your help in positioning me to do so.

**#14** I want to thank Allen Iverson for drawing so much attention to our team during my time with Georgetown. You were able to overcome so much adversity just to enroll in college. I knew early on that no defensive scheme would stop you or contain your potential and destiny. I was happy to see you represented as the number one pick in the 1996 draft and later entering the Basketball Hall of Fame.

**#15** I want to thank my Georgetown professor, Father Raymond Kemp, my photographer, acting, and improv Professors. You all offered me insights that aided me in amplifying my personality on the NBA stage and beyond.

**#16** I want to thank Commissioner David Stern and Adam Silver for welcoming me into the NBA family and giving me numerous opportunities to represent the league and its commitment to communities domestically and internationally.

**#17** I want to thank Kim Bahoney for inviting me to participate in NBA Basketball Without Borders. By allowing me to contribute to the NBA's international success, you've helped me spread my influence around the globe.

**#18** I want to thank Grant Hill for welcoming me into the NBA and sharing what it takes to be an NBA franchise player.

**#19** I want to thank Silas Cheung and Mike Graham and all my high school teammates, for helping to pad my assist stats. When our high school coach shifted his focus toward all of us, it would serve as a critical shift in my role. Ultimately, it aligned me with my NBA path.

**#20** I want to thank Diallo Nelson and Don Deaton for teaming up with me at Montgomery College and showing me how some great players are often overlooked. You both also helped me see how junior college would be our springboard to the major universities.

**#21** I want to thank Damon. Jahidi White, Boubacar, Godwin, Ya Ya, Brendan, Chico, Don, Othella, George, Joseph, and Victor. Each of you helped to push me to become a next-level player, and I will never forget our time together and the moments we spent surviving the coach's practices and high expectations. You brothers have each gone on to do some amazing things, and I am so happy that we all have won in the game of life.

**#22** I want to thank my Uncle Burnett, Uncle Oddie & Uncle Lang for teaching me about the family business of laying concrete and the construction trade.

**#23** I want to thank my Uncle Craig for a special memory I have from elementary school. He lifted my spirits by taking me across town for a basketball game I would miss due to not having a ride. I didn't think I did well in the game because we lost, but you helped shift my perspective on learning from the experience. That was a game-changer. The "We don't lose, we learn..." was born.

**#24** I want to thank my Uncle Oddie, who would take the time to deliver me and my teammate's food when I attended Georgetown University. You were my uncle's app before there became an Uber Eats

**#25** I want to thank Detroit activist and my 1st volunteer Jason Tinsley for assisting Johnnie and me with serving youth.

**#26** I want to thank you for taking the time to engage with my story.

> *We can't ever say thank you enough, but we can leverage the gifts we've been given to win."*
>
> Jerome "JYD" Williams

**#27** I would like to thank Rick Mahorn for mentoring me during my rookie year and just making sure I was at work on time (3hours early).

**#28** I would like to thank Grant Long and Rick Mahorn for the junkyard dog nickname they attached to me.

**#29** I would like to thank Steve Coleman, Mr. Fingaz and Paul Cole, who always kept it positive and made sure I had the right song on my playlist.

**#30** I would like to thank Jerry Stackhouse for the rough edges in practice. He would give his life as a teammate. But his unwavering ability to go as hard as possible.

**#31** I would like to thank some of my Toronto Raptors teammates, including Vince Carter, for the highlights. Morris Peterson for all the three-point daggers. Alvin Williams for his boogie- ball handling, as we used to call it. Antonio Davis for his baseline money shot. Charles Oakley for meals that he would prepare for all the players. And Dell Curry for inviting me to rebound for his young son, Stephen Curry.

**#32** I would like to thank some of my Chicago Bulls teammates: Jamal Crawford for his uncanny ability to create highlights; Eddy Curry for being a fun-loving big man who could drop step with the best of them; Tyson Chandler for just being a great guy, blocking shots and being a tenacious athlete; and Kendall Gill for being that solid veteran.

**#33** I would like to thank the owner of the Toronto Raptors, Larry Tanenbaum, for being a true friend. I will always appreciate the way he treated my family.

**#34** I would like to thank Steve Mills, from the New York Knicks, for becoming a dear friend and helping to bring me to New York.

**#35** I would like to thank Isaiah Thomas for showing me the business of basketball through a different lens.

**#36** I would like to thank Joe Dumars, my teammate in Detroit, for showing me how to transition from a player to a front-office executive.

**#37** I would like to thank my New York Knicks teammates, Tim Thomas, Kurt Thomas, Stephon Marbury, Penny Hardaway., Allan Houston, Moochie Norris, and Nazi Muhammad for exciting MSG.

**#38** I would like to thank all those playground guys. I grew up playing against. We would go at it for hours, and I owe you guys my gratitude for helping me reach the next level.

**#39** I would like to thank Bryan Burrell, whom I met after retiring from the NBA. He helped me solidify the Shooting for Peace Program and so many other things related to my filming businesses. Bryan sacrificed countless hours of dedicated work to help me sustain my brand initiatives.

**#40** I would like to thank Doug Lee and his wife, Becky, for helping me with branding, extending my brand, and helping my son with his brand.

**#41** I would like to thank Eric Broadway Jones for helping me with Shooting for Peace in a way that's unrenowned as our announcer.

**#42** I would like to thank Charles "Choo" Smith for helping me not only become an extended adopted brother but also with Shooting for Peace and the way that he moves with teaching young people to live it, learn it, love it, lead it, and take the initiative.

**#43** I would like to thank my brothers Johnnie and Joshua Williams for all they've done throughout my career and the abilities that they've helped me maintain and achieve throughout our lives.

**#44** I would like to thank my children, Sherae, Gabby, Giselle, and Jeremiah, for just being who they are: hard workers. The work they've put into their lives continues to make me proud, so I thank them for that.

**#45** I would like to thank Lindsey Hunter and Michael Curry, who invited me to team chapel before each game. I went on to include it as part of my pre-game routine throughout my whole NBA career.

**#46** I'd like to thank my big brothers Patrick Ewing, Alonzo Mourning, and Dikembe Mutombo. You three brought the NBA to me each summer as I got an early taste of the intensity I could expect in the league. I felt a lot more prepared for my role and to accept my role because of your mentorship.

**#47** I'd also like to thank other NBA vets like Charles Oakley, who shared much of his rebounding knowledge and wisdom with me.

**#48** I'd like to thank Oshea "Ice Cube" Jackson for reserving a role for me in his Big3 professional league.

**#49** I'd like to thank Harvey Catchings, who spoke with me at the NBRPA Summer vacation and shared his words of wisdom with me.

**#50** I'd like to thank Adam Silver for showing me how the league operates and for keeping me involved with many great NBA initiatives over the years.

**#51** I'd like to thank Arnie Kander, one of the most amazing trainers who helped build the foundation for a durable body. You taught me how to care for mine in a business where the body is vital.

**#52** I'd like to thank John Lucas, my draft combine coach, who said, Jerome, play your game.

**#53** I'd like to thank Alvin Gentry, another coach who let me expand my game.

**#54** I'd like to thank Lenny Wilkins, who was an excellent mentor and the first coach to tell me that if I did not shoot the ball, he was going to take me out of the game; that was music to my ears.

**#55** I'd like to thank Pastor Benny Perez for coaching me in faith and how God's word endures forever..

**#56** I'd like to thank Pastor Bill Alexan for your Basketball Sports Power Team.

**#57** I'd like to thank Pastor Love and all the NBA chaplains for their amazing pre-game messages.

**#58** I'd like to thank the NBA Cares Vice President Todd Jacobson. I appreciate you giving me opportunities to see the world.

**#58** I'd like to thank Charlie Rosenzweig for sharing and always picking up the phone to call me with various opportunities.

**#59** I'd like to thank all the Georgetown alumni who have helped me throughout my NBA and post-NBA career.

**#60** I'd like to thank Samuel "Mook" Mormon for supporting our community efforts around Chicagoland. You are truly an urbanologist with deep insights into ways to spark change.

**#61** I'd like to thank WNBA Legend Merlyn Harris for all the counsel on how to keep my marriage strong.

**#62** I'd like to thank my Findlay Prep players, Kelly Oubre, O'Shea Brissett, Dillon Brooks, Jonah Bolden, Craig Victor, Justin Jackson, Cory Joseph, Tristan Thompson, Nigel Williams-Goss, Anthony Bennett, and Christian Woods, for allowing me to coach them and also Mr. Cliff Findlay for hiring me as head coach of Findlay Prep.

**#63** I'd like to thank Derrick Coleman for giving me a huge assist in helping me obtain my future wife's telephone number.

**#64** I'd like to thank my Woods Academy classmate Jodie Shoemaker for her continued support throughout my career, hiring me as the 8th grade head basketball coach and for helping to assist Jeremiah at Woods Academy.

**#65** I'd like to thank Eric Walters for inviting me to co-author three (3) books together.

**#67** I'd like to thank Jim Williams for putting me in the driver's seat of my Ferrari dream car and for many years of friendship.

**#68** I'd like to thank the Dallas Chapter President Willie Davis for tagging me as the Moses of the NBRPA and always supporting me.

**#70** I'd like to thank Roger Mason and Clyde Drexler for welcoming me into the Big3 and then hiring me as the president of the Young3 to oversee the youth initiatives.

**#71** I'd like to thank Coach OJ for hiring me as a player development coach at St. Albans and always being there for my son.

**#72** I'd like to thank the NBRPA chapter presidents, Tom Hoover, Tree Rollins & Dale Ellis, for always embracing the Shooting for Peace program in their Chapter cities.

**#73** I'd like to thank Rick Darnell and Major Jones for backing the Shooting for Peace initiative in Los Angeles and Houston.

**#74** I'd like to thank former President George Bush for inviting me to the White House twice for dinner.

**#75** I'd like to thank Paul Shapero & Ron Rubin for the constant awareness of financial literacy of my own finances. Not allowing me to become another NBA statistic gone wrong.

**#76** I'd like to thank Stan Mitchell for all of his help in growing my impact in the community long after I had stepped away from the NBA.

**#77** I'd like to thank the Iceman George Gervin for being a dear friend and somebody I can call whenever I needed someone to talk too.

**#78** I'd like to thank Dave Bing for being a true example of transitioning from basketball into business and being a true friend.

**#79** I would like to thank Damon Ford for training and managing my early days in the NBA. Each shot we put up paid off in the long run.

**#80** I would like to thank Junior Bridgeman for being an example of how to manage life after the ball stops bouncing. Your success in business is an amazing example of what is possible.

**#81** I would like to thank Spencer Haywood for pushing what players could achieve on and off the court. Your story has so many layers, and the many sacrifices you endured made things better for players coming after you.

**#82** I would like to thank Julius "Dr. J" Erving for serving as a true role model that I could aspire to play like. Your encouraging words planted hope into my mind when I needed it most. And I truly believed that the NBA was possible when I heard you tell me you would see me there one day.

**#83** I would like to thank my cousins in my Ballard family. We are a large group so I won't name all 86 of us so if your reading this, know I appreciated your support.

**#84** Willie Norwood (RIP) The events I hosted throughout the Detroit community would not have been the same without you showing up to support my efforts to serve. You let me know that the retired legends were proud of what I was attempting to do, and that inspired me to do even more.

**#85** Lorenzen Wright (RIP) The loss of one of my brothers from my 1996 NBA draft class was tough to hear about, my USA roommate.

**#86** I would like to thank Rick Clark for believing in my "Family Business" TV show vision and propelling it to the next level.

**#87** Malik Sealy (RIP): The coolest teammate I could have asked for, and I will always miss your laugh and endless jokes.

**#88** Bill Russell (RIP) The master teacher who led by examples of what excellence looked like and the sacrifices it would require.

**#89** Kobe Bryant (RIP): The most passionate ball player I had the opportunity to play against and get to know while our daughters played volleyball.

**#90** Dikembe Mutombo (RIP) The humanitarian who guarded the basket like a true warrior.

**#91** I would like to honor **Dennis "The Worm" Rodman,** whose passion paved the way for me to emerge from college as a high-energy ball player with an inviting personality. Before there was a Junk Yard Dog, there was the rebound legend of you. Thank You!

**#92** Thanking my guy Robert Smith for taking me on the investment banking school for athletes and creating a dream team called SEE Fund.

**#93** Thank you to Chuck Williams for opportunities in television production that put me in position to utilize my talent.

**#94** Thank you to Brother Revin from Chicago for all his advice and assistance he gave my brother Johnnie about the history of Chi-Town basketball.

**#95** Thank you Greg Hymowitz for your support of my "Shooting for Peace" tour in NYC schools.

**#96** Lastly, I must thank God, my Lord and Savior Jesus Christ for all he has done in my life and continues to do. #JesusWins

*"If you have read this chapter and did not see your name, I want you to know that you are appreciated and that my wonderful life experiences also reflect your fingerprints."*

# The Family Business

*"Jerome, when we teamed up as your parents, we both accepted our roles to nurture and raise you. Our job was to coach you into a young man who could make wise choices and win at the game of life."*

Dad and Mom

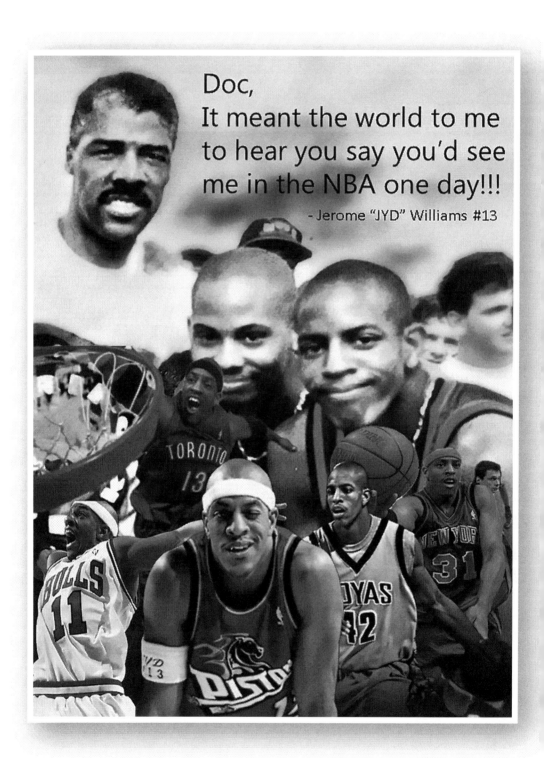

Doc,
It meant the world to me
to hear you say you'd see
me in the NBA one day!!!

- Jerome "JYD" Williams #13

# NBA Awards

- 2005 – NBA Community Service Award
- 2003 – NBA Community Service Award
- 2002 – NBA Community Service Award
- 2000 – Fannie Mae Home Team Award
- 2006 – Awarded Letter from the President Bush Administration for service to youth across the US
- 2005 – Proclamations from cities including Detroit, Las Vegas, Toronto, New York, New Orleans, Memphis
- 2024 – White House Panel in Chicago

# Community Service Contributions and Clinics:

- 2005 & 2006 –2 trips to the White House for his Community Service under Bush Admin
- 2000 – 1$^{st}$ NBA Ambassador to China, and NBA Ambassador to Beijing
- 2000 – Present – NBA Global Ambassador
- 2002 and 2015 – Basketball Without Borders – China, Shanghai
- 2003 and 2004 – South Africa – Basketball Without Borders
- 2003 – Was the Botswana NBA Ambassador
- 2009 – Canada, Calgary – U.S Sports Ambassador 09' Envoy
- 2011 – Bahrain- U.S Sports Ambassador Envoy
- 2012 – Became NBA Fit Ambassador
- 2013 – Present – Became Las Vegas Chapter President
- 2007 – 2014 – Was a Findlay Prep Volunteer Coach for 7 years and Head Coach of the 2013 Season with over 13 NBA players graduated

- 2015—Started Shooting for Peace Programs, which raised $1.9 million in Scholarships from HBCUs for high school students. The program is currently servicing over 35,000 students in the USA and is ongoing.

- 2017 –Voted NBRPA BOD

- 2018 – Became President of Young3.org; a BIG3 Program dedicated to giving youth more opportunities to play 3-on-3 basketball

- Started the Williams Endowment Montgomery College Scholarship Fund, which has gifted over 35 scholarships to local & International students

- Dedicated over 50,000 hours Dedicated to Community Service through the JYD Project, Positive Shades of Black, NBA & NBRPA LV chapter

- Authored Student Financial Literacy, Reading, Health, and Fitness books & programs

- Made over 1000 Hospital, orphanage, and school visits

- 2024 Shooting for Peace Update; Over $10 Million in scholarships awarded to youth throughout the USA

## Sports Ambassador Trips

- 2007 – Philippines – JYD Project Ambassador

- 2009 – Israel- Sports Power Ambassador

- 2010 – South America- Basketball Without Borders

- 2011 – Bahrain – U. S. Sports Ambassador

- 2012 – India – Sports Power Ambassador

- 2015 – Belarus- Sports Power Ambassador

- 2015 – Shenzhen, China – NBA Ambassador

- 2016 – Mexico City, Mexico – NBA Ambassador

- 2016 – Beijing, China – NBA Ambassador

- 2017 – Shanghai, China – NBA Ambassador

- 2017 – Nigeria, Africa – NBA Ambassador
- 2017 – Bafokeng, South Africa – NBA Ambassador
- 2017 – Haida Gwaii, Canada – NBA Ambassador
- 2017 — Saskatoon, Canada – NBA Ambassador
- 2017 — Newfoundland, Canada – NBA Ambassador
- 2018 — Beijing, China – NBA Ambassador
- 2018 — Montreal, Canada — NBA Ambassador
- 2019 — Rwanda Africa — NBA Ambassador
- 2023 — US Ambassador (8) Military Base Tour Africa, Middle East & Cuba

## Basketball Highlights

- 1993 – Became JUCO State MVP
- 1995 – Lead Big East Conference in Rebounding
- 1995 - Big East All-Conference
- 1995 – Selected to USA Men's College Team
- 1996 – Made Elite 8, Big East All-Conference
- 1996 - NBA 1st Round Draft pick
- 2000 – Led NBA in offensive Rebounds- Top 10 in NBA
- 2001 – Runner-up 6th Man of the year
- 2017 – Finalist BIG3 Defensive Player of the Year

## TV Show Highlights

- 1999-2005 – NBA Inside Stuff Correspondent
- 2005 – NBA TV Analyst
- 2006 – "Make it Hot" on MSG Network
- 2010 – The Basketball Channel
- 2024 – "Family Business" on PlayersTV Network

# Coaching Resume (Findlay Prep)

- 2008 – Volunteer Coach – Avery Bradley and DeAndre Liggins
- 2009 – Volunteer Coach – Tristian Thompson and Cory Joseph
- 2010 – Player Development Coach – Nick Johnson and Jorge Guertez
- 2011 – Assistant Coach – Anthony Bennett and Christian Wood
- 2012 – Associate Head Coach – Nigel Williams-Goss
- 2013 – Head Coach – Kelly Oubre, Rashad Vaughn, Dillon Brooks, Jonah Bolden, O'Shae Brissett, Justin Jackson, and Craig Victor
- 2013 – National High School Tournament (Final Four)
- 2018 — Assistant Coach for BIG3 Champions Team Power
- 2018-2024 - President of the YOUNG3 for Big 3 league
- 2021 — President and Owner of Las Vegas TBL franchise
- 2023 – Head Middle school Coach ST Albans in DC.
- 2024 – Head Middle School Coach Woods Academy

"*My respect goes out to all of the role players who may not have been widely celebrated. I know our individual and collective impact has been felt.*"

Manufactured by Amazon.ca
Bolton, ON

45380573R00101